SEXUAL
INTELLIGENCE
IN BUSINESS

SEXUAL INTELLIGENCE IN BUSINESS

BOBBI BIDOCHKA

Copyright © 2020 by Bobbi Bidochka.

All rights reserved. No part of this publication may be reproduced, distributed, or transmitted in any form or by any means, including photocopying, recording, digital scanning, or other electronic or mechanical methods, without the prior written permission of the publisher, except in the case of brief quotations embodied in critical reviews and certain other noncommercial uses permitted by copyright law. For permission requests, write to the publisher, addressed "Attention: Permissions Coordinator," to the address below.

ISBN Paperback: ADD # 978-1-7774648-0-6
ISBN Electronic: ADD # 978-1-7774648-1-3

Library of Congress Control Number:

Portions of this book are works of nonfiction. Certain names and identifying characteristics have been changed.

Bobbi Bidochka
www.SexualIntelligenceInBusiness.com

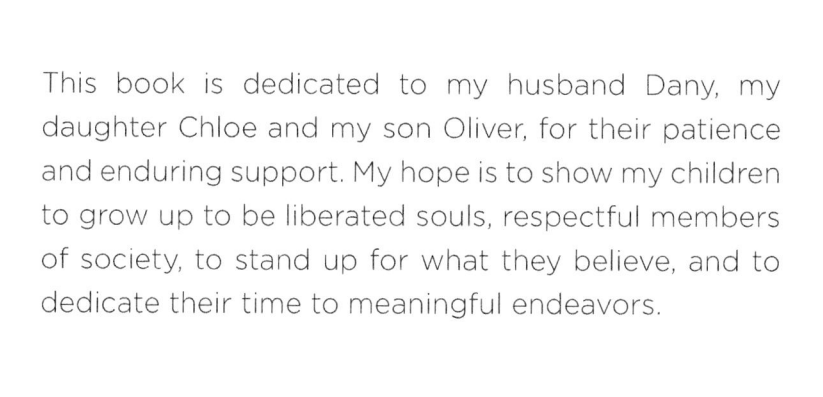

This book is dedicated to my husband Dany, my daughter Chloe and my son Oliver, for their patience and enduring support. My hope is to show my children to grow up to be liberated souls, respectful members of society, to stand up for what they believe, and to dedicate their time to meaningful endeavors.

Table of Contents

Introduction xi

Preface 1

Acknowledgements 7

The Chronicle: Cultivating Change 11

Sexual Intelligence In Business: The New Framework 29

Sex And The Workplace 51

Second Order Consequences Of #metoo 65

Power, Patriarchy And Perception 85

The Freedom To Negotiate 103

Identity Irreconcilable Differences 125

Altered States And The Science Behind Productivity 145

Femme Fatale: Vice or Virtue? 169

Looks Matter, Especially In Business 177

Harness Erotic Capital And Sexual Transmutation.. 191

The Beginning..207

Bibliography.. 211

SEXUAL INTELLIGENCE IN BUSINESS

INTRODUCTION

Over the past ten years, there have been interesting developments in business. Entrepreneurship is exploding, people think it's super sexy, and it seems that everyone wants to be a CEO. Everyone wants a piece of the pie or to get their five minutes of social media fame. A peculiar consequence of social media is that it gives people a false sense of what it takes to be successful, alluding that it's easy and accessible and everyone has the skills and abilities to be the next Elon Musk or Oprah Winfrey. Along with that, there has been a proliferation of coaches and experts selling get rich quick business programs and self improvement silver bullets. When push comes to shove, not everyone will have the dedication and gumption to stick it out, because it doesn't happen overnight. One must face reality that building a business and entrepreneurship is hard and there is an onslaught of obstacles with constant uncertainty. At the same time, not everyone wants to hold a c-suite position. And that's ok. Some people are quite happy with a position in a company that pays the bills. Either way, if you do think you have what it takes or you do want to advance in your career, and you want to equip yourself with every

Introduction

possible tool in the tool box, then read on. Upping your game with Sexual Intelligence for Business will not give you overnight sexcess. But what I can say is that if you overlook this very important skill set, you risk losing out. Because the one thing we all have in common, one way or the other, is sex, which makes it on of the most important things in the world.

There are a few things that make the human experience of this world go around. Love, sex, power and money. It can be argued that everything else stems from those. Everything we do, every action we take, is in service of those four concepts. What is the ultimate point of obtaining power and money, to acquire resources to stay alive, to flourish? It is so we may have love and sex. As much as we can possibly get our hands on. Start looking around and see how much people want to touch, want to make a joke, want to pay a compliment, want to have more fun, be more flirty, but are so uncomfortable now. There are important and relevant reasons for this, which will be further explored in this book.

What we can see now, is a futile attempt to separate love and sex from money and power. With the increase in technology, automation and globalization there is a lot more business creation and much more office jobs. There has been a feeble attempt to separate work from personal lives and most people find this hard because the best work environments are those where we have good relationships with our colleagues. To have good relationships, this involves the personal. After the #metoo movement, this attempt of entirely eliminating love and sex has been in full force but it will not work well. In this book, not only will I attempt to show that this is an impossible feat, but also an undesirable one. What's more, I strongly believe we should bring them all closer together than ever. We are doing ourselves and humanity a great disservice by trying to extinguish sex because there are enormous benefits to receive and opportunities to enjoy. We are by nature, sexual beings and social creatures. Relationships are extremely important, professionally and personally.

Like anything in this world, there is often a dark side.

- Falling in love and terrible breakups.
- The invention of transportation increased our mobility dramatically, but also sometimes results in fatal car and airplane crashes.
- The benefits of our new technology age and those who use data for nefarious purposes.

The list goes on. Unfortunately, what I see with sex is that, because of its taboo reputation, people often focus on the dark sides, like sexual harassment and sexual violence, instead of all the great and wonderful things about it. If it wasn't for sex, you wouldn't be here! My hope for this book is that, we start to embrace all the great things about sex, and bring about a new sexual era, a sexual glory days. I would

Introduction

like to begin those glory days right here, right now. In this book, I will present to you ways in which we can make that happen and why it is so important that we do that.

This book contains a substantial amount of research, an assemblage of advice and how-to's, a Sexual Intelligence in Business framework, intermixed with some humour and sass. Most of the topics are well-known, highly investigated and written about in great details by many others. As you will notice chapter by chapter, I give examples of other authors or experts who delve into each topic in far more depth and I encourage readers to go ahead and learn more about those topics from those authors. If I tried to cover all these topics in depth, this book would be 10,000 pages and nobody would read it! This book is unique in the sense of putting all these ideas and notions together, and linking them to business by developing a framework that is practically applicable. I do present some provocative notions, and I do hope to spark some discussions from that. I'm very open to respectful feedback and I'm even more open to alternate opinions and ideas. This book is not the be-all-end-all, but more of a conversation starter.

Some say I'm a problem solver, but really, I'm a problem finder, a gap see-er. What I do well, is curate and make sense of situations, bring clarity to otherwise muddy rivers, in a meaningful and relevant way. At the intersection of sex and business, things are unclear, there is some confusion, apprehension and after many conversations with people, it seems there was an underlying concern about how things are going in this post #metoo era, but a fear in speaking out about it. I wrote this book, as a reaction to the second order consequences of the #metoo movement. It was not my career aspiration to become an author, that's why I refer to myself as an accidental author. I really felt compelled to write this book, and to express both my opinions and reflections from conversations I had with a diversity of individuals. I did not conduct official opinion polls or personal interviews, but rather have brought together an aggregated collection of conversations, distilled and intermixed with my own opinions. What I can tell you for sure, not one person strongly opposed or thought completely the opposite, which hints that there's something here. Many admitted that they would be afraid or concerned to express them publicly. I know for certain there are many people who will unequivocally disagree with every word in this book. Nonetheless, I tried to cover themes that I thought were relevant. Most likely I overlooked certain aspects, there will be ideas and concepts that I did not consider. I welcome anyone to point those out and open those conversations. Perhaps together, we can arrive at bigger and better ideas and solutions.

In this book, you will be presented with a brief historical lookback on sexual revolutions and feminist/womens movements, to ground the conversation. I will discuss how sex is playing out in the workplace, from affairs to

Introduction

human resource policy (in the western cultures). I cover the #metoo movement, and its second order consequences that have arguably in some ways resulted in an additional and new barrier to women's advancement. I present to you some concepts on power, patriarchy and sexism and how those intersect with business. One extremely important thing to point out, is this is from a western perspective. Not only is the "problem" a western one, in terms of women's equity, the ability to vote in a democracy, equal wages, but most of the "famous" sexual harassment/violence cases are heteronormative. Having the opportunity or the environment of which we can be more sexually expressive and inclusive is also most accessible in western cultures. In addition, the LGBTQIA2+ has its own unique struggles when it comes to equity, diversity and inclusion issues, along with dealing with sexual harassment and sexual violence in a multipolicy of ways that white westerners simply do not have to face. Because I'm a western woman and my impetus for writing this book is in direct relationship to the #metoo movement, it is indeed from white heteronormative perspective. Having said that, I went to great efforts to use inclusive language, because I do believe the Sexual Intelligence in Business framework can be applied to everyone. It really is customizable. I will also take this opportunity to invite anyone from the LGBTQIA2+ to reach out to me and discuss these topics directly and my hope is that can inform a more inclusive and widely applicable framework in future editions.

Along this journey, you will learn a few techniques on how to integrate sex and negotiation and apply those in both the bedroom and the boardroom. I share my critique on 'identity' as well as a surprising and empathetic defense of men. I take issue with a new form of sexual repression of women through the femme fatale lens and then move into, what appears to be a contradictory chapter on how looks matter. Then we have some real fun in exploring all the ways sex is awesome, beneficial for your health and even more beneficial for your business!! I achieve this by outlining the science behind neurochemicals and informing you on a strategy called erotic capital.

To help bring it all together, you will be presented with a framework and set of principles that I'm calling Sexual Intelligence in Business. This is based on intertwining the concepts of IQ, with components from Emotional Intellgience, Sexual Intelligence and Erotic Intelligence. I've adapted from those ideas to come up with a new one that applies to your career and business. Here's a sneak peak:

Sexual Intelligence in Business framework:

1. Constant Consent & High Levels of Respect
2. Own Your Body - This is Your Power Source
3. Empathy & Awareness
4. Moderate Irrational Emotions emotions
5. Education & Learning

Introduction

6. Open Communication & the Liberty to Negotiate
7. Grey Thinking: Sex is Equally Serious & Fun
8. Capitalize on Sexual Energy

What will you lose if you don't start thinking about Sexual Intelligence in Business? Opportunity to change for the better, business and career success, freedom to be yourself, and being healthier and happier.

There's a few ultimate goals here. We need to change minds, not just change behaviors. We need to start operating from a collective and systemic approach. We cannot achieve results like eliminating sexual harassment and sexual violence without working together as human beings. I also strongly believe that, although gaining voting rights, pay equity, and women in leadership positions are all great things, we will never truly achieve parity until women (and men also) own their bodies. We need to stop looking at sex as taboo (because surprisingly, it's actually not) and start to embrace all the wonderful aspects that are available and that means bringing it out into the open in new ways. Yes, sex is everywhere in film, television, mustic, art, etc But we still experience shame and apprehension when it comes to expressing ourselves and sharing opinions, in places that really matter. Sex is so much more than orgasms and reproduction. It encompasses physical health benefits, mental health benefits, its a source of power and energy that is not to be underestimated. Sex is ubiquitous, it is in everything. If we hope to dismantle the patriarchy system, we have to develop something to replace this with. We can only achieve that together. We need to stop shaming women and blaming each other and ourselves. It's time to adopt an open and growth mindset when it comes to sex and business. This will benefit society, this will benefit the economy. We need to create space for diversity, for choices and freedom of expression.

From an educational perspective, my hope is that the information, tools and point of view provided will help people to become more aware of themselves and situations, to give permission to flirt and find love in the workplace and business, to clarify some confusion in environments so that people can feel more comfortable being themselves. I would love for men to learn about consent, learn about women's historical struggles and adopt more respectable behaviors. I would love for women to have compassion towards the learning journey that men are on. I would love for men to teach other men and stand up for women when women are not in the room. Most of all, it would be amazing if we could learn what it means to be sex-positive and sexually intelligent, not as an identity, but as an action.

What we are really talking about here, is power and its many meanings. Most people, when they think about power, they think of authority and law. They think about institutions and people that exert authority and have the ability to punish. And yes, of course, that exists. However, we underestimate the origins of power. We think less about, unfortunately, the existence of power as a force, power in the more ambiguous forms, in the abstract form, as an internal activity, as a life force. Power, as a force, only exists when there are opposing elements. Power is something that is channeled and exerted, when there is a pathway for it to move between. By definition, there needs to be a plurality, multiplicity and contrariness involved. It is a process, and component to an ongoing social structure.

For example, Foucault's writes about the link between power and knowledge. That power is converted, that works through people rather than upon them. He also claims belief systems gain strength (and hence power) when people accept those views associated with that belief system as common knowledge. When that begins to occur, belief systems define their figures of authority, such as medical doctors, academics or religious leaders in a place of worship. When the discourse (or sanctioned knowledge that can be 'known') is crystallized with right and wrong, or what is normal and what is deviant, then any contrary views, thoughts or actions become unthinkable. These new undeniable "truths", come to define a certain way of seeing the world, and the specific way of life associated with such "truths" becomes normalized. That is how power works.

Although subtle, this form of power lacks rigidity and other narratives can contest it, as we have seen with the #metoo movement. Indeed, power itself lacks any concrete form, occurring as a site of struggle. Resistance, through defiance, defines power and thus becomes possible through power. In modern times, we are consistently at a precipice when it comes to social movements. Sexual Intelligence in Business could be one of those bridges that can help overcome these crevices we've created for ourselves or a channel to which power can move, shift and be adequately resisted in ways that are more productive.

When you read on through the chapters, you will notice that in the chronicle, for example, there were certain points or sites, where power shifted, by a particular resistance. In the chapter on sex and the workplace, you will see how HR and/or leadership is trying desparately to control the situation but you can also see how, the psychology of scarcity actually will make this effort moot because when you try to make something scarce, people start wanting it even more. When discussing more themes throughout the book, how to destroy patriarchy when there is no site to move that power to, and how you can take back your sexual power. With any great changes, you can expect to receive resistance. My hope is that we can see power as a source of energy and discover the ways in which we can rearrange it. Lots to be learned here. Views to be undone, and new discourses and belief systems to be formed. Let's start with Sexual Intelligence in Business.

Sexual Intelligence should be a respectable characteristic as is artistic creativity, athletic ability, business savvy or engineering ingenuity. With this book, we can provoke conversations, you can discover how to empower yourself and enhance your business. You will be better. Others will be better. The world will be better.

PREFACE

I write this preface as a declaration. I am not a scholarly academic, I do not hold a Phd in Sexology and I am not a certified sex therapist. Most authors who write non-fiction have some academic authority position to lean on. Most of these authors have many great and valuable things to say, speaking from many years of study in their field. But not everyone who writes a book necessarily has spectacular things to say. As you will see throughout the book, I conducted a ton of research and I credit those investigators for providing me with the research that can back up my assertions. Without research, this book would be entirely editorial. I would like the readers to be informed, enlightened, and inspired. Maybe even delighted. For this process to occur, we need a nice mix of academic research and a way to link all of that research together in a theme that makes sense and that readers can learn, grow and improve their lives.

My background is extremely varied. When I say extreme, I mean that quite literally. I have heard time and time again, and through my own experience, that my background is quite unique. This has afforded

Preface

me a perspective and knowledge base that is both extraordinary and horizontally broad. I grew up in Regina Saskatchewan, into a family that had its fair share of problems, divorces, marriages, sexual harassment cases etc. I was promiscuous from an early age, I've had a ton of boyfriends, and other encounters in all sorts of configurations. I was shuffled around a bit from family member to family member, teenage pregnancy, drug abuse, etc. I also started working very early, I had my first job at 14, but I was working in my Dad's shop from the moment I could turn a screwdriver. I spent my twenties moving around, city to city, job to job, looking for something, looking for myself, as it were. When I was 30, I moved to Montreal, finally finished a degree in Political Science, got married, had children. By the time I was 40, I had moved forty+ times, with nearly forty different jobs, having attended eight different schools and worked in nearly every sector. Finance, retail, hospitality, sales, IT, corporations, non-profits, government, the arts, academia, the startup world and venture capital. I often get two reactions to this. People think I jump around and don't commit. It is true that I did jump around, but I wasn't about to stay anywhere, when I knew that, this wasn't "it". I had no intentions on giving up on myself and settling for something that wasn't what I wanted. The other reaction is awe, how did you manage to jump sectors and still do well? How did you get the courage to move to cities where you knew nobody? The answer to this is less succinct. I don't know, I just did. I'm a quick study, I love learning, I make friends easily and at the end of the day, no job is really all that complicated when you try your very best. The reason why I'm telling you all of this is first, to show not everyone needs to go on a neat, linear pathway through life. It also shows, and I hope that some of this is inspiring, to not stop until you find what you are looking for, despite the pressure you feel from society to conform. Lastly, to demonstrate that not all knowledge is acquired at school. Life experiences teach us something too.

But where the page turned for me, was when I started to pursue my long time dream of starting my own business. I've probably had 20+ false starts. I've lost count of the amount of times I tried this or that. When I looked back at all the things I did, and could see a common thread. When I reflected back, it all clicked. This is literally where 'hindsight is 20/20' kicks in. When I started doing research for this book, it felt so comfortable and so right, like this is what I was meant to do. When I started my company, and taking on the projects and events that are aligned with my values, everything was starting to converge on a common goal. "Moving ideas forward."

Ever since I've started developing and growing my business, one thing has become strikingly clear. Your network is your net worth, as they say. I did not grow up in Montreal and so I did not have historical ties and lifelong relationships to rely on that others do. I had to start making connections, basically from scratch.

Preface

Whether I was building my business or working professionally, I was confronting many of those obstacles that women face, bias, microaggressions, discrimination, judgements, imposter syndrome, etc. I've been at this for a while and yes, things are changing. There is much more awareness, especially after the #metoo movement. I still face these regularly. Woman-only in the boardroom, paid less for just being female, and assumptions about my intelligence based on my hair colour. When I have a conversation and then I get the 'surprise' reaction that I'm "actually smart". People literally say this, "oh wow, you're really quite smart". Insert head shake here. The list goes on. The difference between me and most, it may be that I speak up more. I point things out. I also send a very clear message, don't fuck with me. Unless I want you to.

I also send another very clear message, I like flirting, I like compliments, and I like sex jokes. I have never been sexually harassed, I've never been offered a promotion in exchange for sex, not literally or figuratively. I've never found myself in a situation that I could not handle. I believe this is because a) my openness to sexual expression mixed with b) my confidence, attitude and ability to tell people to fuck off and c) my sexual intelligence.

We cannot succeed in business and do great things without mentors. You need people on your side. You need people in positions of power. Guess what? They are mostly men. I'm totally down for dinner and drinks.

Why? Because that is where the magic happens, that is where relationships are built. Breaking bread and spending time. Meetings, sometimes closed doors, yes, that's right! Right now, many men are concerned and so they want to avoid precarious situations. But not with me. My message is so darn clear, there is no issue for anyone. There is no chance of misinterpretations. The men I encounter, that I collaborate with, that I seek out mentorship with, are solid, super respectful, nice and properly ethical. I do not see this as an accident. Right now, mentorship with men is compromised, because of the second order consequences of #metoo.

Bit of a rant there, I know. The point here is to say that, because of this type of lived experience, I have a holistic vantage point, it has shown me how to link things together in a way that others had not thought of, or at least not written about. For sure, most of the information in this book is not created by me, nor does it need to be. There are several books on each individual topic. As far as I know, it has not yet been put together in this particular way before. My goal was to put this all together, in a way that gives people a practical way to move forward. It's great to have feminist theories, but how do we as societal members, outside of academia, apply that in everyday scenarios? It's even greater to have loud advocates, on social media and in Hollywood, but how does that trickle down into practical applications? And it's even more critical that we have high-level officials creating policy

Preface

and changing laws, but those policies are reactionary. We need proactive and preventative solutions. Now.

I believe in sex-positive feminism, I have a voice, I have ideas, I'm speaking up. That is what is required here. You can do it too.

ACKNOWLEDGEMENTS

First, I would like to extend my deepest gratitude to my parent, family, friends and colleagues for their support. Most especially the grace I have received in attempting to tackle controversial topics addressed in this book and asking themselves, how the heck did I end up writing about sex! I would also like to thank everyone who supported me by pre-purchasing the book, that really meant a lot to me.

I would like to thank and acknowledge the amazing contributions of my publishing consultants, Kristen Wise and Maíra Pedreira from PRESStinely. Without your guidance and knowledge, I would not have this beautiful product which I'm very proud of. I'm super grateful for your positivity, enthusiasm, passion for publishing and just seeing your happy beautiful faces every week. I would say I'll really miss that but I've been so inspired by the process, I've got two more books to write. This is just the beginning!

I would like to give a very special thanks and ultimate gratitude to my husband Dany and my two young children, Chloe and Oliver. Every minute I spend on

Acknowledgements

the book is a minute I'm not spending with you. I greatly appreciate the sacrifice you have made and the relentless support you gave, and continue to give, as I embarked on this journey to authorship.

A very special thanks to Tony Tkalec, who without your friendship and encouragement, this book would not exist. An opportunity came to help another friend out with their book, together with Tony, and I thought it might be a good way to see what that would entail. Through the meetings on that project, conversations, and philosophizing with Tony about metoo, society and our culture, I came to realize that I had something to say. He strongly and continually encouraged me to write this book. It was through his coaching and constantly pushing me for updates and chapters and being a solid soundboard on the content, that I was able to keep going and finish the book, despite the obstacles. I've said many times, no Tony, no book, and this is the truth. For that, I am eternally grateful.

Lastly, I would like to extend my greatest thanks and heartfelt acknowledgment to my business partner, Amanda Chalupa. In fact, she is so much more than a business partner. She is my co-conspirator, my interlocutor, my academician, my intelligentsia. Never have I had a relationship with a female that is so compatible and complementary. She thinks of things that I don't, she brings a perspective that is fresh, wise, different, and yet harmonious. We debate and philosophize with levels of respect unbeknown to me historically, she is the yin to my yang. Without Amanda, imagine ideation would not be in existence and thriving and her support of me in writing about sex has been unwavering, as she has dived down into the rabbit hole with me, unabashed. She is my closest friend, she is family, she is everything anyone would ever want beside them. If I achieve any level of success in this world, it will be a direct result of my relationship with her. Without her, I am nothing.

CHAPTER 1
THE CHRONICLE CULTIVATING CHANGE

Sexual Ideologies and Feminist Movements

I want to begin by grounding the book from an established basis of ideologies and movements. Historically, there was plenty of significant events like the conversion to an agrarian society and industrialization. But also, some recent turning points greatly affected sex and gender. It's essential that we take a step back and look at what has occurred historically, even if only briefly. There are many outstanding academics and well-versed advocates who know the history full well. But for the rest of us, we may only know bits and pieces from what we've heard over time, perhaps mostly sound bites in the media, movies, or television. We cannot take for granted that readers might not have in-depth knowledge, even if we care about the subject. There is so much to know. Everyone cannot be an expert, and that's ok. At the same time, it is beneficial to have a baseline of knowledge to come to our own conclusions, instead of exclusively borrowing opinions from others. We often do this for the sake of efficiency. It is part of how our human brains can manage all the information. These days, we take in more knowledge, images, and information in one day than most people did in their entire lifetime, historically. There's a lot of noise, a lot of opinions. Many of us now rely on social media to present us with news and information, but the algorithms defy us and give back to us the things we like, which causes confirmation bias. We must also expose ourselves to ideas and opinions that we disagree with, which oppose our values and beliefs, that call into question our thinking line. This is an important consideration to help us make informed decisions. The topics in this book are too important not to consider and reflect on. Through this reflection, we can begin to identify the parts that we can apply to our lives and reap its benefits.

To that end, this chapter presents a brief summary of sexual ideologies in modern times and women/feminist movements. Because a considerable impetus for me in writing this book was my reaction to the #metoo movement and its subsequent second-order consequences, I think it's important to ground the conversation and start from a foundational point. It is also my assumption that many men are not as familiar with feminist movements as women are. I wrote this book for everyone, and so in service to that, a look back is valuable. This summary is not a complete history from beginning to end. The situation, execution and reactions to sexual ideologies and feminist movements vary from country to culture. Still, this look back provides just enough information to understand better how we got here. There also may be some surprising and interesting nuggets that everyone can enjoy.

Who controls sex and the pursuit of love? Is it man or woman, or does it have little to do with gender? Are we all merely lemmings unable to do anything but follow the pathway to love by giving in to our sexual wants? Or do we have some agency here? How much choice and authority do we really have regarding our bodies, sexual desire, or quest for love? Alain de Botton, a Swiss-born British philosopher, and author, wrote in his book *Relationships* that "love has a history, and we ride – sometimes rather helplessly – on its currents." Is it that simple? To delve into today's issues surrounding sex, the conundrum of what is acceptable, and if sex and business can mingle together in the boardroom, let's revisit the recent history of love and sex in western culture.

The Enlightenment Period Of Sex

The Age of Enlightenment was a European philosophical, free-thinking intellectual movement of the 17th and 18th centuries centered around reason and individualism over tradition. This enlightened liberal movement made its way from the study to the boudoir, rebutting earlier religious beliefs and removing constraints that held a stranglehold over sexual practices. Society started to tolerate certain heterosexual sex acts outside marriage, including prostitution, mistresses, and pre-marital sex. Infidelity became a civil matter and no longer a criminal offense punishable by capital punishment.

One of the results of this acceptance of promiscuity? The rate of bastard babies (yes, an ancient and outdated term that refers to children born out of wedlock) jumped one percent in 1650 to about 25 percent in 1800, with around 40 percent of brides being pregnant. This statistic is a staggering increase of pregnancies outside marriage that speaks to two things. One, people like having sex, and there is a need for birth control options. It's hard to say how much of that sex outside marriage was coercion instead of chosen or sought out by women. But I think it's safe to say that this was the dawning of a new day where women started to take control of their bodies. Masturbation, homosexuality, and rape were oddly less tolerated. Under an Anglo Saxon point of view, I suppose so long as they were procreating, the 'outside marriage' part was more acceptable of other avenues of sex that were simply based on pleasure. Visiting a female sex worker was seen as a reasonable recourse for a man (of course) to release pent-up desire instead of masturbating or nevermind having a homosexual encounter. Authorities began reacting to the increase of the individual's sexual license by curtailing sexual behavior variations with regulations. These regulations led to an odd juxtaposition of heightened sexuality with a newer rigidity towards acceptable social norms. You could be a freak but only in specific and sanctioned ways that society and the government dictated. Even today, homosexuality, masturbation, owning a sex toy, etc., are illegal in some places in the world.

The Enlightenment came to a close and onto 19th-century Romanticism. An ideology that reached its peak from 1800 to 1850 in Europe when poets, artists, and philosophers took the stage in the theatre of love and sex, for some, as they philosophized and manifested ideas about beauty, sensuality, and the like. They took an introspective approach, one that focused on emotions and the sublime, convinced themselves that love conquered the world, and these notions still resonate today.

During this period, we also start to see how this romantic approach became integrated into science, literature, politics, and identity. Eroticism started to appear in medical dictionaries during the Romanticism era. Eroticism is a philosophical concept surrounding desire, sensuality, and romantic love; it often manifests itself through artistic mediums and literature.

The Victorian Era – Disease, Pornography, Masturbation

It's so interesting how, from era to era, the pendulum swings. The Victorian era was the era of buttoned-up social manners. Prim and proper. One of the main contributing factors for this straight-laced reality was the spike of Syphilis in the world. The fear of disease made sex a dangerous activity because Syphilis was spreading rapidly, peeking around every bedroom door and every corner. The 1800s was the century of sexually transmitted disease, and so it made sense to override sexual urges. Syphilis was considered a Godly punishment for loose morals; nothing like fear to get people in line.

The Victorian era itself reflects the period of 1820 to 1914, part of which was dominated by the reign of Queen Victoria in Britain. There was a prudish refusal to admit the existence of sex, hypocritically combined with constant sex discussions, thinly veiled as a series of warnings. People wrote about sex. Erotic literature was proliferating along with pornography, medical treatises, and psychological studies. Most "respectable" people never talked about sex; instead, they gossiped about the sins of those who did, thus, the early beginnings of modern-day slut-shaming. People even talked about not talking about sex! In that vein, in his book the History of Sexuality, Michel Foucault thoroughly crushes the argument that society was sexually repressed. Just the opposite. I would argue the same situation exists today.

The Petting Party (snugglepupping) The Roaring 20s

World War I changed the social landscape and brought an end to the Victorian Era. Women gained more social power due to having to step up and take charge while men left for war. This power inspired women to seek out social freedoms and break free from old society rules.

In the roaring 20s, petting parties became established. These petting parties were a safe way to experiment without going the distance to full on intercourse and dealing with the ramifications of pregnancy, STD's or moral implications, like loss of virginity. Oh, how dare she lose a commodity like virginity? Much of the condemnation about petting parties focused on the young women's supposed immorality. "The boys of today must be protected from the young girl vamp," complained a New York mother to the New York Times in 1922. As you will see in subsequent chapters, this idea of protecting males from female sexuality is a recurring theme, one of which I take major issue. There is an inverted paradox that lives here. Where men, who are supposedly the strong, smart, leaders and yet, are the ones who require protection. Conversely, women were considered weak, not smart enough to vote, not actual persons, are the ones to be protected from? So who is strong or weak? Who is the protector and the protectee?

Who are these Girl Vamps? Known as Flappers - with their short hair, shorter dresses, makeup, and participation in drinking, smoking, and dancing - were free spirits and countered many traditional notions of femininity and "appropriate" behavior for women. Their participation in "snugglepupping" was an extension of this, but they weren't the only women taking part in public petting.

In general, women at petting parties engaging in activities were considered by their elders as amoral and impure. The pious and the feminists threw around words like vulgarity, revolting badness, and rapid moral decline. The Women's Christian Temperance Union spoke out against them as did the ultra-conservative League of American Women in New York. These groups tried to limit the contact young men and women had with one another, usually unsuccessfully. A significant game-changer in the roaring 20s was the accessibility of motor vehicles because now there was somewhere private to go. As automobiles became increasingly widespread, this opened the car doors to the backseat. Coincidentally, before the 1920s, 86 percent of women were virgins before marriage. After the 1920s, however, the number fell to 61 percent. Correlation or coincidence?

Women also took off heaps of restrictive clothing. Forget about the layers and long horse shit-stained dresses. Thank you, Coco Chanel, for the newly-popular fashions in Paris. Hemlines rose, and necklines plunged, and short haircuts, painted lips, and silk stockings ruled the day. It was a new era for women. She worked and voted. She smoked, drank, and danced. Who was to blame for this modern, scandalous young woman? Ironically, the first woman in congress, Oklahoma Representative Alice Robertson, accused mothers. She alludes that if a mother went out of the house, say to play a card game with friends, leaving her slutty daughter unattended, well....then it's only natural the daughter would dash out of the house and into the first back seat of a car she could find! These attitudes are the harbinger of the future. It is hard to hear and realize that there are women historically, and now, who prefer to maintain the status quo, and thereby preserving patriarchy. More to come on that topic.

Kinsey In The 1950s

In 1950, biologist and sexologist Alfred Kinsey chimed in with his Kinsey Report. As a pioneer in the field of sexology, Kinsey was a biologist by training and a professor of entomology and zoology. In 1947 he created the Institute for Sex Research at Indiana University. His seminal work, Sexual Behavior in the Human Male (1948) and Sexual Behavior in the Human Female (1953), resulted in what is now known as the Kinsey Reports and the Kinsey scale. Kinsey's research on human sexuality, foundational to the field of sexology, naturally provoked controversy in the 40s and 50s. His work has been influential on both social and cultural values in the US as well as internationally. He notes the "petting parties" of the 1920s had altered the way men and women engaged in sexual contact.

The Industrial Revolution And Fast Change

The Industrial Revolution during the 19th century and with the growth of science and technology, medicine, and health care, resulted in better contraceptives. There were advances in rubber manufacturing and rubber production, resulting in the design and production of condoms that could prevent pregnancy at minimal cost, relatively speaking. Progress in chemistry, pharmacology, and biology led to the discovery and perfection of the first oral contraceptives, popularly known as "The Pill."

In 1960, when the birth control pill came on the scene, this finally gave women access to safe and reliable contraception (thank you, John Rock, a gynecologist, reproductive biologist Min Chueh Chang, and Gregory Goodwin Pincus, a biologist responsible for the pill's development). It was precisely May 9, 1960 that the US Food and Drug Administration (FDA) approved the first commercially produced birth control pill in the world. Birth control activist and founder of "Planned Parenthood", author, nurse and all around Feminst Superstar, Margaret Sanger initially commissioned "the pill" with funding from heiress Katherine McCormick. Germany was the first European country to legalize the pill in 1961. Most European countries followed suit shortly after that. Canada was pro-contraceptive back in the 30s, but it took until 1969 to legalize the pill in Canada. Having some semblance of control in regards to reproduction was a major contributing factor to women's liberation. This occurrence is not to be underestimated. Another recurring theme in this book surrounds the idea of 'choice'. Or more succinctly, the freedom to choose. It is my strong opinion that once people (yes, not just women) own their bodies, fully, this is when we will reach equity. Also beneficial for women was a vast improvement in obstetrics, significantly reducing the number of women who died during childbirth, thus increasing women's life expectancy.

A further liberating factor was the medical discovery of penicillin. Since this discovery significantly reduced the mortality rate in Syphilis, this, in turn, sparked another increase of sexual escapes during the mid to late 1950s, unmarried, married, extra-marital, and various other compositions. Subsequently, divorce rates were dramatically increasing, and marriage rates were decreasing. People began to realize they could redefine marriage by instilling new open marriage institutions, mate swapping, swinging, and public sex.

In 1966, the established "morality" in the US was shaken when *Memoirs of a Woman of Pleasure*, better known as Fanny Hill (a mound of Venus), was written in 1748 by John Cleland, considered the first pornographic novel in English, was released. Cleland reportedly wrote the story in debtors' prison in 1748, his imagination in overdrive. Yet, he wrote this book without using a single "foul" word. The novel was banned in both the UK and the US until 1966 but banned in Singapore until 2015. Framed as two letters written by Frances "Fanny" Hill to an unnamed "Madam," the novel recounts the fictional Fanny's experience as a prostitute starting at age 15. This book has been published in many different versions, under various titles, including Memoirs of the Life of Fanny Hill, or the Career of a Woman of Pleasure.

In 1963, Putnam published a new edition of *Memoirs of a Woman of Pleasure*, leading to the arrest of New York City bookstore owner Irwin Weisfeld and clerk

John Downs, the unfortunate victims of an anti-obscenity campaign orchestrated by several political figures. The battle became known as the ban of Fanny Hill. Weisfeld's conviction was eventually overturned, as was the prohibition.

The new edition was also banned for obscenity in Massachusetts after a mother complained to the state's Obscene Literature Control Commission. The Massachusetts high court ruled Fanny Hill as obscene, and the publisher's challenge to the ban went up to the Supreme Court. In 1966, the United States Supreme Court ruled six to three in Memoirs v. Massachusetts that Fanny Hill did not meet or exceed the standard for obscenity and was protected by the First Amendment. This opened a door; the genie was out of the bottle now. What is also a bit daunting, 1966 is not that long ago! This speaks to the rapid changes (I'm purposefully not using the word 'progress') that we have experienced in the last sixty years, relative to history.

First-Wave Feminism 1848 to 1920

In the late 19th to early 20th century, first wave Feminism was formed and fought for causes such as voting rights, health, labour, political and legal equity. (Western) Feminist activists mobilized and organized themselves to reform a society that was dominated by the White Middle-Class male. It is important to remember that these early women's movements were super courageous and diverse and frequently held conflicting agendas amongst activists, not to mention the conflicts between feminists and female citizenry in general. It is also essential to consider that the early feminist movements were mostly white women in North America and some of Western Europe. This was an early example of both the potential and challenge of creating broad-based coalitions that attempt to unify groups and take on issues that try to serve broad categories. This is a never-ending battle that, in my opinion, is a challenge to resolve.

On August 18, 1920, the US Constitution was ratified granting voting rights for women, also known as "The Susan B. Anthony Amendment" in honor of her work on behalf of women's suffrage. First-wave feminists, suffragettes, used to be called "special interest groups." Still, all groups and points of view, whether of class, race, religion, or ability — undermined a unified activism project. Ultimately, the struggle for women's rights or Feminism never attracted all women. Some women wanted to opt-out altogether. Unfortunately, at the time, feminists considered any non-feminist, promiscuous, or otherwise, as an impediment to the movement. Even though feminists pursued causes and issues that, in the beginning, had poignant campaigns and advocates for significant changes and were supercritical to the evolution of women's movements, it was hard to imagine that all women wouldn't want that.

*Second Wave Feminis*m 1963 to the 1980s

Second-wave Feminism redefined sexuality, not only in pleasing men but also in recognizing women's sexual satisfaction and sexual desire, was a thing. From the women's movement came lesbian Feminism, freedom from a heterosexual act, and freedom from reproduction. An essential figure in the Feminist movements, Betty Friedan, published a book titled, The Feminine Mystique in 1963, that outlined the many frustrations women had with their lives and how separate spheres (home vs. work) established a pattern of inequality. Her book and her activism is not to be underestimated. She is credited for starting the contemporary Feminist movement.

During the second and third waves of Feminism, women's liberation was often equated with sexual freedom rather than associated with it. Meaning, even though there were still several items and issues on the docket, women's sexual freedom took precedence. At that time, many feminist thinkers believed that assertion of the primacy of sexuality would be a powerful approach towards the ultimate goal of women's liberation. Thereby, women were encouraged to initiate sexual advances, enjoy sexual pleasure, and experiment with new types of sexuality.

The US Supreme Court decisions of Roe v. Wade and Doe v. Bolton that decriminalized abortion nationwide in 1973, was a very pinnacle moment in liberating women's bodies and reproductive choices. Although abortion is legal, there is still much, not must controversy and many attempts to repeal the law. In 1967, the United Kingdom legalized abortion and Canada in 1969. Many countries in Europe followed suit thereafter, but with varied circumstances and conditions. What is important to note here, is that restricting abortions doesn't actually reduce the number of abortions that women have, but it does dramatically reduce women's safety, if they are compelled to pursue an illegal, and more importantly, non-medical abortion. What has reduced the number of abortions is access to contraception.

The feminist movements insisted and focused on the sexual liberation for women, both physical and psychological. The pursuit of sexual pleasure for women was the core ideology, which subsequently was to set the foundation for female independence. Despite the progress made and freedoms gained during the 1960's sexual revolution, many feminists felt that the lived experience mostly played out in favor of men and at the expense of women. For example, the increase in sexual liberation and the decrease in monogamy exclusively manifested itself with men using many more women for sex, 'pumping and dumping' you could say. This gave men notches in their bedposts and left women feeling used. Maybe the timing was off then, but I feel like now is an excellent time to get back to this agenda. It is my point of view that this is a narrow outlook because sexual liberation does not necessarily mean women seek out copious copulation in order to feel sexually free. There are several other ways that people can experience sexual freedom and liberation without intercourse, necessarily. Control over our bodies, over women's reproduction, non-hetero configurations, just being comfortable to speak about sex, seek out and receive adequate medical care, and equally important, self-pleasure.

Third-Wave Of Feminism 1919 -

The third wave of Feminism emerged as those born in the 1960s and '70s came of age. This generation of feminists enjoyed the benefits of legal and voting rights achieved by their predecessors, but there was still a lot to accomplish. Although criticized for their white middle to upper-class privilege in the US, they started pursuing sexual division of labour, sexism itself, racism, and classism. They were dedicated to supporting groups and individuals working towards gender, racial, economic, and social justice, and the concept of intersectionality became imperative. During this era, the US Equal Pay Act that prohibited sex-based wage discrimination was signed on June 10, 1963. As well, on July 2, 1964 the US Civil Rights Act was signed in that banned employment discrimination based on race, religion, national origin or sex. Major significant moments here.

Influenced by postmodernist philosophy (social constructions and individualism), third-wave feminists questioned language and ideas about womanhood, gender, beauty, sexuality, femininity, masculinity, etc. During this period, perceptions of gender and challenging natural born characteristics defined as strictly male or female, embedding the nature vs. nurture debate into feminist theory. They expanded the idea that sexual liberation involves a process of discovering how gender identity and sexuality are shaped by society and then, by extension, reclaiming that process to construct one's own authentic gender identity.

Fourth-Wave Feminism

Starting around 2012, the fourth-wave feminist movement began with a focus on sexual harassment, body shaming, and rape culture, among other issues. You can see over time how many issues needed addressing and how these topics have evolved. The movement has grown over the following years, bringing condemnation to dozens of powerful men in politics, business, entertainment, and the news media. #metoo also inflamed contemporary criticism inherited from third-wave Feminism in relation to misandry, which is the visible and invisible hatred of men, blaming all men for current and historical patriarchal institutions and systems. This philosophy, of man-shaming, I believe, will impede progress.

So now we're up to speed. Each period and movement of yesteryears left an imprint on our sexual reality of today. Let's step into the boardroom now and see how this all intersects with business.

CHAPTER 2
SEXUAL INTELLIGENCE IN BUSINESS THE NEW FRAMEWORK

What is Sexual Intelligence?

In order to gain the benefits and have the best experience reading this book, I invite you to view the presented information, knowledge and opinions through the lens of Sexual Intelligence. Several components make up the technology of sexual intelligence in business. When we understand and embrace this framework, there is potential for transformational experiences. Let's walk through how I came to the Sexual Intelligence in Business framework.

First, what is intelligence? This word is often equated with being smart or educated, but those two words have different meanings, albeit nuanced. Being "smart" means you have an ability to learn and may have a quick-wit intelligence. Whereas being "educated" implies something more formal. Meaning, you've gone through an educational program or institution, that has by some mechanism, granted you an academic credential; a certificate, diploma, degree, etc. Going one step further, by definition, intelligence is the ability to learn or understand or to deal with new or trying situations, the skilled use of reason and the ability to apply knowledge to manipulate one's environment or to think abstractly. We often only consider the negative side of the term *manipulate*, but in this case, it's the practical version.

Throughout modern history, there have been several attempts at measuring and classifying intelligence.

Pioneer in psychometrics and statistical methods, Francis Galton, was the first to have a go at creating a standardized test. Several others continued this type of work. It was German psychologist William Stern who coined the term IQ, for Intelligence Quotient, in his work on standardized testing. Of course, these tests have come under scrutiny, being biased in many different ways, including by gender, culture, location, economic status just to name a few.

Then we have Emotional Intelligence. Originally discussed in the 1976 paper, *The Communication of Emotional Meaning* by psychologist Joel Robert Davitz and clinical professor of psychology in psychiatry Michael Beldoch, this term became popular in 1995 in the book titled Emotional Intelligence by Daniel Goleman. The time was ripe. During this period, global capital markets became increasingly integrated, prospects were super high, world trade expanded strongly, globalization was unstoppable. Indeed, the money and opportunities were flowing, but that created a very competitive environment. Superior leadership and management performance became top of mind. It was no longer enough to have a great product or idea. You gotta be awesome too. Skills and abilities in emotional intelligence became another aspect of competitive advantage.

What is Emotional Intelligence? Many people are already quite familiar with the framework. Daniel Goleman and Richard E. Boyatzis have produced valuable literature that we are all encouraged to review. I will briefly point out a few things just to ground the conversation.

The basics are that emotional intelligence can be organized in four domains:

- Self-awareness
- Self-management
- Social awareness
- Relationship management

Within these four categories are several subcategories that include: emotional self awareness, emotional self control, adaptability achievement orientation, positive outlook, empathy, organizational awareness, influence, coach and mentor, conflict management, teamwork and inspirational leadership.

Many people have a good grip on some aspects of these subcategories, but it definitely takes an intentional and concerted effort to become aware, acquainted, and skilled at not just randomly exercising them, but knowing when and where to do so. I read the Emotional Intelligence book nearly ten years ago and I'm still honing those skills. Like everything else in life, there isn't that *one thing*, that is the be-all-end-all. But when you put all the pieces together, a set of accumulated, aggregate knowledge, then you've got something.

Some think there is a dark side to emotional intelligence. More precisely, the skill of reading people. Indeed, with everything, there are ways to use things for good or evil, famous examples such the Hitler or Machiavellian types who use their skills to manipulate others for strategic and evil ends. Yes, it is important to keep in mind that not everyone acts in good faith. But this is inescapable and one could make that same argument for pretty much everything. I caution those who continuously look for nefarious intentions. If we look for trouble, we will find it.

Now we have Sexual Intelligence, proper. Academically trained in Sociology, and Certified Sex Therapist, Dr. Marty Klein wrote a book titled Sexual Intelligence: *What We Really Want From Sex and How to Get It* (2012). In his book, Dr.Klein explores what he considers to be the fundamentals to a better sex life. In opposition to more orgasms, better techniques, and process oriented solutions we find in mainstream media, Dr. Klein describes a more mature approach to sex. He outlines his three tenets, and the how to's, that includes 1) Facts and Information (one must seek education about sex); 2) Develop Emotional Skills to navigate better sex and; 3) Awareness of our bodies (or more to the point, acceptance of our bodies). He says that Sexual Intelligence is "the ability to keep sex in perspective, regardless of what happens during sex, to get more out of sex. We have to change, we need a different perspective and Sexual Intelligence is that perspective". Dr. Klein goes into depth on many of the psychological barriers we put in place for ourselves. Now you can see, it is easy to start drawing that line between sex therapy, IQ, and Emotional Intelligence principles. Again, much like with Goleman and Boyatzis, Dr. Klein does a very fine job at explaining the details of his approach in his book, which I also encourage everyone to read. I wanted to touch upon the main concepts to explain how there's a pathway towards linking sex and business in ways that may not have been thought of before. The idea here is to allow us to start connecting the dots as we move forward in the journey of exploring what is Sexual Intelligence in Business.

Next we have Erotic Intelligence. This is a concept coined by Esther Perel, a self-proclaimed psychotherapist who, in her book, Mating in Captivity: Unlocking Erotic Intelligence (2006), where she explores the tension between the human need for security (love, belonging and closeness) and the need for freedom (erotic desire, adventure and distance) in relationships. When we think about 'erotic' we sometimes giggle and think about naughty photographs, torrid erotic novels, or subjects we think are on the fringes of 'normal' sexuality. What the word actually represents is desire, etymologically based from the Greek word, eros. The word erotic embodies the concept and ascetics of desire and sensuality, perhaps even capturing arousal and impulses. What is more interesting and relevant here, is that Eros has often been equated with "life energy". This life energy that is equated or produced, is topic we will further explore in the coming chapters. Esther draws our attention to the dilemmas of desire, the tragedy of not getting what we want, and the tragedy of also getting what we want. She touches on some very relevant topics. For example, in western society, we are extremely discursive (you'll see more of this subject in the Chapter on Power), we are constantly talking and disclosing every detail in our minds, a "hegemony of talk" as she notes, as a way of transcending our internal selves. We are asking our partners/spouses to be everyone and everything to us, we ask of one person that which an entire community used to provide. She further explores this existential tension between safety versus novelty, the erotic versus the domestic. There is an aliveness and vitality in eroticism that we crave and need. In our quest for transparency, and to be known, we relinquish the mystery and captivating qualities we need for desire to flourish.

When we think about business or work, imagine a time when you've had a job or task that was routine. Like ultra routine. You show up, to the same place, sit at the same desk, Monday to Friday, 9am to 5pm. You perform the same job and tasks, day in and day out, with very little variety. Without a doubt, there are some folks who appreciate the security, the predictability, those who work to live. To pay the bills, not as interested in self-fulfillment. Which is fine. If that is what you want. For most of us, I would argue, we don't want that. The best positions or jobs are arguably those that are dynamic, where we encounter challenges, changes, new people, and a variety of activities and tasks. Taking that to the next level, for those who are business leaders, founders, entrepreneurs, these roles are even more dynamic, high risk, filled with uncertainty and are very invigorating. There are major goals to be accomplished, not just the roles involved but also the significant impact of being cultivated and shared. Simultaneously, operating at these levels, taking on the responsibility of big business, leading teams, of multi-million+ budget where competition is fierce, hours are long, and challenges are steep. We need all the extra energy and help we can get. The desire for dynamic activities goes far beyond the bedroom and envelops every aspect of our lives. The thing is, we often spend more time on business and work than anything else and so you can start to see how the same concepts that promise amazing sex, can provide the same outcomes at work and in business. There is a positive feedback loop here. The better sex or self-pleasure you have, the better your business may be. The better business you have, the better sex you can have! When we can apply the same concepts that we know about Emotional Intelligence and Sexual Intelligence and apply those to business and the workplace, that is the next level.

Sexual Intelligence in Business Framework and Principles

1. Constant Consent & High Levels of Respect
2. Own Your Body - This is Your Power Source
3. Empathy & Awareness
4. Moderate Irrational Emotions
5. Education & Learning
6. Open Communication & the Liberty to Negotiate
7. Grey Thinking: Sex is Equally Serious & Fun
8. Capitalize on Sexual Energy

Throughout this book, we can begin to understand how sexual energy and vitality can be applied to business by learning about how, for example, the neurochemicals produced by our brains when we experience everything from a compliment, to a crush, to a romantic affair to full on sexual intercourse, can be useful to produce a state of mind that is more productive and creative. We can apply the knowledge that we learn from reading people, as a way to navigate the business environment in a post-#metoo era. Coming from a place of knowledge and empathy, when we educate ourselves about the importance and outcomes of sexual revolutions and women's movements, along with the #metoo movement's original purpose, we can better understand and respond to sexually charged situations in business and the workplace.

How do we do that?

Sexual Intelligence in Business Framework and Principles - Let's flesh these out a bit

Constant Consent & High Levels of Respect

We all have different levels of comfort, expectations, preferences and tolerance. We come from different backgrounds and have different life experiences. Although genetically, humans are 99.9% identical, that picks up enough variation that is both delightful and has potential to cause issues. This is part of why consent is important. The idea of consent, as we are referring to it here, stems from the idea of 'Age of Consent', which is the legal age at which a person can make sexual decisions for themselves. This varies from country to country. The age of consent in most Western countries is between 14-18 years. Since the #metoo movement, the idea of active consent has become much more important, no matter what age you, because people are afraid to speak up. It's easier to say yes or no.

As a society, we need to get better at both implicit and explicit consent. Most people believe consent is important, but there isn't agreement about what it means. And we are not going to solve that here. But there are signals we give and signals we receive and usually these are obvious. When it is not obvious, this is where we need to, as uncomfortable as it may be, ask explicitly for consent. However, we cannot stop there. It is one thing to ask, it is another to formulate a respectful response, which is what most of us would like to do instinctively. Easier said than done, especially on the fly. But what about the person receiving a rejection, how do we teach to receive and respect that rejection? When you employ high levels of respect, what tends to follow is empathy and tolerance. Meaning, if someone is trying to give consent or trying receive consent, we must also help them along with that. Until things are more systematic, we should be gracious with our efforts. We have to be very intentional here. Being aware of consent is the place to start. Engaging in consent conversations is next, practice makes perfect.

Own Your Body - This is Your Power Source

Your body is yours and yours alone. Nobody has intrinsic rights to your body. Tragically, human bodies are abused and violated in various ways around the world. But in our hearts, we have to know, for ourselves, that our bodies are ours. It is my strong opinion that until women own their bodies, in their mind, in their heart, in their relationships and legally, nothing else we do in this struggle will move the needle. You would be surprised how many women, in western countries, where this approach is available to them, still do not realize this. Most men have historically owned their bodies, and you can see how well that works! Again, let's not generalize here, there are men in this world that historically and today, do not and have not owned their bodies. Gay men, men who are smaller in stature, or considered "weak" by male standards, or "emotional", people with disabilities, etc. There is a struggle in this aspect, for everyone. But it's the key. And I'm not just speaking of legal or political ownership, which is indeed very important. What is the body for? The body is a container of your life energy. There are power systems outside the body and there is a power system inside the body and people don't use it! Sex is the most optimal channel to which we can harness your energy and power. We need to be in the driver's seat, making decisions for our body. The better we eat, the better our body operates. When and with whom we reproduce, or not. Where we go, who we have sex with, who we let touch us and how we touch ourselves. Every decision we make for our body impacts our day, the people around us, how we feel, how well we produce in society, how far we can reach, how many of our goals and dreams we can realize. We highly underestimate the sexual power source we have available to us. No More! With Sexual Intelligence, we can elevate and transform our life and business.

Empathy & Awareness

This is an extension of respect. We have to give a shit about people. This is where we put ourselves in someone else's shoes, where we imagine how we might feel. We have our own reactions to things, but we also need to consider others. If we are an empathetic lover, this means our partner's pleasure is as important, if not more, than our own. This is something that is taught by many sexuality coaches or sex therapists, and its also surprising to know how many people are not empathetic and lack awareness for their sexual partner and for their own sexual desires as well. The good news is that it can be taught. This plays out in Sexual Intelligence in Business, by helping to understand for example, who we can flirt with and who we should not, who we make sex jokes with, who we might have a crush on. For example, someone might have a tramatic past experience that our sexual advances are provoking, and not in the good way. Moreover, they may not want to reveal that to us either, especially if we are a colleague or client. The reasons why someone rejects our advance could be so varied, and might have really zero to do with us. So don't take it personally. At the same time, showing empathy is a great bonding mechanism, and so it can work in both directions in a positive way. It's good for you and it's good for humanity. Especially in a world where greed and duplicity tend to show up in the same places where money, power and influence also do.

Empathy only works if we have the ability to be aware. Being kind to ourselves and kind to others stems from an understanding of the self. There is something called self reflection, that many people avoid because it's uncomfortable at first. For example, after a full day of work, whether you are a cashier at a store or a CEO of a global corporation, going home and reviewing the day, what happened, what was said to you, what you said to others, how people reacted... this can be hard. A lot of the time, we'll be looking back on mistakes. Things we regret saying. Things we wish we had done differently. Things that others said or did that we're now bent about. In many cases, we want to ignore it all. Because it hurts. But that is where the gold is!! If we don't reflect on our actions and those of others, then we have no chance of correcting. Then we are destined to just keep repeating and experiencing the same mistakes, the same shit, over and over. This is pure suffering. It does get easier. Once we figure out to look at it objectively, instead of beating ourselves up or blaming the other person. If we look at it from a different point of view, and ask ourselves "what could I do differently, how could I improve on that, and then actually try it"? Over time we'll see the results. And so will others. When I was in high school, there was the girl, who most people were afraid of, because she would kick your ass. Well, she didn't like me. One day, she was threatening me. Once it became known that she wanted to beat me up, I was afraid to go back to school. I went home crying and my Mom gave me the best advice that I still use to this day. You can't change other people's behavior, but you can change your own. And when you change yours, others are forced to react differently. And so I did. And wow did it work. From that day forward, I just kept evaluating myself and changing. Constantly. It has served me well. When you pay attention to yourself, others and your surroundings, you get a TON of information, that is said and unsaid. Never close your eyes to that. It's all gold.

Moderate Irrational Emotions

You may have noticed that I've used the word 'moderate' instead of control. The reason for this is because I don't think it serves us well to consider it in those terms. Using 'control' gives the impression that we should hide or be shameful of our feelings, to shut them down, block them out, etc. That is not at all what I'm proposing. Instead, becoming aware of our emotions means understanding when is the time to address them and in what way. It is not in anyone's best interest to lash out, explode, go off the rails. This tends to not go well in personal relationships and its sudden death in business and the workplace. Moderation is required. They call it "professionalism". But when we are involving sexual feelings, that consideration becomes all the more important. As you read through the book, you will see how workplace affairs and the chemicals our brains produce can go south if you are not prepared. If you want to use Sexual Intelligence in Business to its maximum benefits, you will need to get a good grip on this. How each person goes about this, would be a bit different and this goes back to understanding and learning about yourself, becoming self aware, recognizing your boundaries, both physical and emotional, and respecting that.

Education & Learning

This one is pretty obvious. I don't think anyone will argue that learning more and gaining more education is a bad thing, as a concept. What is shocking to me is how many people avoid it, because it takes effort. The fact is, knowledge is power and so if you are seriously interested in advancing your career and/or building a killer business, you must be on a constant learning track. There are many ways to accomplish this, especially these days with so much access to books, online classes and education being accessible to most, in western countries. The same goes in the bedroom. If you educate yourself on techniques, learn what the other person likes, implement open communication and listening, then you will, unequivocally, have better sex. Same for using Sexual Intelligence in Business. We have to learn other people's sexual tolerance map, by listening and paying attention. How far can we take that sex joke, even if we have no interest whatsoever in having sex with that person. How comfortable are they going to a business dinner with you, what is happening after one glass of wine, are things going in the wrong direction? Also, educate yourself on what is sexual energy, what are the neurochemicals going on in your brain that make your body feel the way it does. How long does it last, what ways work best for you to evoke those chemicals? What are your limits? How do you channel that energy into being more productive and creative? You must find out if you want to take advantage.

Open Communication & Freedom to Negotiate

Ask and you shall receive. Well, at a minimum, you could increase your chances. You really need to ask for what you want in this life. In fact, you might need to demand it or even fight for it. One way or the other, you do need to communicate your thoughts, ideas, feelings and requests to start. In the same way that you need to communicate your sexual desires to your partner(s) in order to have great sexual experiences, so the same goes in business. If you want the opportunity, you have to ask for it, you have to go for it. Nothing is going to be handed to you. Rarely do employers offer you gigantic raises, rarely do clients come begging for your business. It's all a hustle. If people do not report harassment cases, nobody can do anything about it. If you are unhappy in your relationship, and you do not communicate that, how can you ever solve any problems? This all sounds very obvious but tragically, it remains an issue. Sometimes this means walking away from a lover or a job or an opportunity, because parties are not getting what they want. Here's the hard truth: if you don't want to have those conversations or ask for what you want, there's a good chance you won't get it.

There would be absolutely no concept of "negotiation" if everyone just got what they wanted without asking. This is an unrealistic and utopian idea. When you think about it, from a mechanical and operational point of view, it's not even possible. There are too many opposing viewpoints. This would quickly slip into chaos and tyranny. In many other parts of the world, one can negotiate, at different levels of society, within the community, family or in individual relationships. In western societies, we have laws and rights, mostly. This framework does afford many people the freedom to negotiate. Again, the problem here is that many people just don't opt in, they choose not to negotiate. There's more about this in the negotiation chapter, but it's really important to note that we negotiate for many things throughout the day. They may be overlooked, but pay attention for a week and reflect on that. The point is, we have the freedom to negotiate, we should take this opportunity, in order to be more successful in our lives, jobs, and businesses. Educating ourselves on basic negotiation strategies and just starting to practice them will help us improve and dissolve some of the related fear.

This is important with Sexual Intelligence in Business because, as you will see in the following chapters, we can harness our sexual energy in ways that can increase our chances of better negotiation outcomes.

Grey Thinking: Sex is Equally Serious and Fun

We know today, how many directions that sex can take us in. This can take us to the absolute best moments and 'pinnacle of life', pivotal life-changing type of experiences. Sex can also get you harassed, violated, thrown in jail or killed. This could be the most crucial indicator of the sheer magnitude and importance of the power of sex. This is where being adaptable and grey thinking becomes critical. Many people want an easy solution, the silver bullet, just tell me the right thing to say or do. Let's erase all sexuality at work and in business and this will solve the problem. But life doesn't work like that. Nature doesn't work like that. Humans don't work like that. Every situation is complicated and simple at the same time. The concept of grey thinking is that we can have an opposing point of view, about the same thing at the same time. Given the times right now and how North American politics for example, seems so polarized, one might wonder, how is this possible? Many folks see things as black or white. As binary. We often like this method, because it's clear and does the thinking for us. Day or night. Light or dark. Hot and cold. The problem is that some people only consider the ends of the spectrum and overlook everything in between. But that messy, grey middle is where most things actually exist. Look at war, as an example. As a concept, most people will say they are against war. But then, there are times where most of those same people understand there is time for it. Especially if you literally have an enemy knocking at your door. It's a bit of a gory example, but it illustrates the point. Therefore, it stands to reason that we can consider the fun and seriousness of sex, all at the same time. This is also why it can be the case, where even in a work or business environment, where sexual harassment and violence are top of mind, that we can still flirt, we can still have workplace affairs, we can still use our sexual energy and erotic capital. We have the ability to hold both, what appears to be opposing concepts, at the same time. We can do this successfully, if we apply the Sexual Intelligence in Business framework.

Capitalize on Sexual Energy

If we do not capitalize on our sexual energy, we are literally leaving money on the table. There is a broad selection of concepts and tools, that we can decide on how much or how little we do apply. We'll need to curate a plan that works for us as individuals. Starting from our mindset and level of self awareness. How well do we know ourselves sexually, how aware are we about how much sexual expression we do naturally, or none at all? How do we feel when we see others expressing their sexuality? Do we judge them, envy them, or relate to them? When assessing the environment we are in, how much of that is influenced by #metoo, our personal experience, our religion or culture? I would recommend spending some time looking over those things and this will give us an idea about how much or how little we can do, within our comfort levels. When it comes to visual appearance and how sexy or not, you choose to present yourself. Not just in the clothes and makeup, but also how you move your body, and how you move in different environments. Because there's a line, of course, of too much. But that varies from person to person and in different environments and scenarios, so you need to make that assessment. Read the room. Then there's the language we use, and what stories we tell. How much sexual terminology, or facial expressions, sex jokes or innuendos, do we utilize, because these also communicate messages. We should be intentional here. Again, read the room. Next is the charm and flirting. We need to assess who we can do this with, and who we cannot or should not. Relationships may form from this, and we'll have to navigate that accordingly.

Now this is all very situational and also we don't need any of this to be produced in these ways, in our professional or business environment to benefit from sexual energy. We can evoke all the best sexual energies without ever displaying outward sexual expressions at all, if we choose. We can have a crush on someone, inside or outside work, a new dating relationship in the honeymoon phase, or we could be having phenomenal sex in any part of our lives that nobody in our professional or business environment knows anything about; we can harness that energy and be super creative on our projects and wicked productive in our business, and totally nailing it. We can even arouse our sexual energy with fantasies or masturbation, nobody else needs to know or be involved. Totally independent. The power resides in each of us. Do what works best for you. We'll dive a bit deeper on these topics in the coming chapters.

One thing that is 100% certain, we cannot shut down our sexuality. You can't. Instead, convert it into something intelligent, that can be useful. Like any good set of tools, best to learn how to use the tools properly, so you can build something amazing.

CHAPTER 3
SEX AND THE WORKPLACE

There could not be a more appropriate time and place to be developing our skills in Sexual Intelligence. Now more than ever, sex and relationships in the workplace and in business are a hot topic. And not just a hot topic to discuss around the water cooler, but critical to the degree that law and policy are involved, people from all sides are being harassed, dealing with discomfort and judgment for filing charges, losing their careers, facing hostile workplace and business environments, even criminal charges. This is serious stuff. Most of which is entirely preventable, if everyone can embrace and apply the Sexual Intelligence in Business framework. People and businesses are reacting in all sorts of ways; there is much concern. Of course, everyone has their own opinion and agenda. All organizations, corporations and entities want to avoid lawsuits, people want to eliminate unwanted sexual advancements and discrimination (disproportionately affecting women), and there is an interest in reducing confusion on all sides. At the same time, whether they admit it or not, people desire to be themselves, people want to live an authentic life, professionally, personally and in the bedroom. We must recognize that we may meet people in business and the workplace that we develop friendships with, romantic relationships, consentual workplace affairs, and even marry. So how can everyone get what they want?

What I'm not going to discuss here are important issue like gender equity, equal pay.

State of the Union

One-third of working Canadians are now or have been romantically involved with a co-worker. One-in-ten office workers in Canada have been in a relationship with a colleague holding a senior position at the same company, and nearly half of Canadians keep their workplace relationship a secret. These are pretty big numbers when you think about it. This is also only based on what people are willing to disclose; you can bet the real numbers are higher. The data comes from a 2019 survey on workplace romance conducted by ADP Canada, a Toronto-based HR consulting firm. Although the Canadian numbers will vary compared to the United States or Europe, we can safely extrapolate some similar conclusions.

Despite workplace romances being quite common across Canada, many employees are still hiding them, which is a good thing given the climate. But it doesn't help with data collection, that's for sure. Keeping on with the statistics, more than 45 percent of those in workplace relationships kept it a secret from someone in particular, and 38 percent of people who have been in a relationship with a co-worker kept it a secret from HR. Also, from the same study, 40 percent of people who have been in a relationship with a co-worker kept it a secret from managers, and 27 percent of those in relationships (current or past) kept it a secret from everyone at the office. These numbers speak to the ability of humans to be discreet and respectful when most of the narrative around town is that when sex is involved, people get crazy and irrational. But given the situation we are in right now, it may be more appropriate to keep things low key, out of respect for your co-workers, and to avoid corporate impediments, but there's also something inside me that wishes we could be more transparent. I'm an advocate for being open; I look for freedom of expression and yearn for the day when love and sex are normalized in the workplace and business. There may be some who are more private, and that is to be totally respected. There are many more who think that by declaring workplace or business relationships, this is out of protection for women, there's debate about that. We can draw on Sexual Intelligence in Business to manage these relationships, manage our own emotions and self-monitoring, develop our organizational awareness, and be more effective.

If you are in a romantic relationship, a purely physical one, or even a close friendship, there are ramifications on both sides that employers and employees need to be aware of. Some HR folks believe that clear policies need to be established and communicated for the protection of everyone. Companies want individuals to document relationships, even if doing so seems un-romantic. This doesn't seem to count for non-romantic friendships, which have their fair share of ups and downs. Can you imagine having to fill out forms and declare a close friendship to your employer every time? I would even go as far to say that tumultuous colleague relationships give management far more grief than sexual ones do! Given that relationships are the foundation of everything, these HR policies seem a bit extreme. Is this really the world we want to live in? And what does this really solve in the end? Other than a safeguard against lawsuits for companies? Or is it a false sense of companies doing something positive towards eliminating sexual harassment and violence. These are important questions and considerations to make to ensure that a safe and respectful workplace is made possible for all.

But is the Human Resource Department going to help you out with that?

According to an article written in 2019 by Caitlin Flanagan in the Atlantic titled, *The Problem With HR: For 30 years, we've trusted human-resources departments to prevent and address workplace sexual harassment. How's that working out?* she states that "HR has been almost universally accepted as the mechanism by which employers attempt to prevent, police, and investigate sexual harassment." But the problem is they don't deal with sexual harassments cases in the way one would expect. HR departments on the whole, have failed greatly at preventing sexual harassment in the workplace, but rather are "serving as the first line of defense against a sexual-harassment lawsuit."

Flanagan further reports that in 2016, a special task force from the US Equal Employment Opportunity Commission (EEOC) released its findings on sexual harassment. The task force found that "Much of the training done over the last 30 years has not worked as a prevention tool," and reveals that sexual harassment is "widespread" and "persistent," and that 85 percent of workers do not report harassment. The task force itself also cited that the evidence shows sexual harassment training does not effectively reduce the frequency of harassment occurrences and that HR tools and training are predominantly focused on protecting the company from liability. What this tells us is that we cannot rely on companies, polices or laws to prevent or protect us. We must take matters into our own hands and in my opinion, that is the way to go anyways. Don't wait for policy and law to catch up with you, empower yourself.

When getting into relationships of any kind, everyone knows the stakes. Shit happens, emotions are present, humans are complicated creatures with 'baggage', which counts in the workplace, in business, and otherwise. You really cannot separate these. It can be hard to know what the true nature of a relationship was in the beginning, even for those who were in it! And even if it began consensually, it could turn into harassment. There have also been cases where people deny that things were consensual, after the fact. There are false accusations; we can't bury our heads in the sand about that. Again, emotions run high; sometimes, people make poor choices and react irrationally. The primary issue with that right now, in this post #metoo climate, it only takes one false accusation to create doubt in real cases. This has significant implications in the worst ways for cases of rape, sexual harassment, and sexual violence. It blows my mind that people don't realize that. Unfortunately, with humans, it doesn't take much to break trust, or hurt egos. It isn't straightforward for people to determine when to exercise that trust and when not to. Presumption of innocence is an essential tenant in the court of law, but this causes issues regarding sexually related cases because it might need to be the other way around. Would it be possible for no presumptions at all?

Often, any relationship between supervisor and subordinate raises a conflict of interest, and red flags, even if they try to keep it professional. There is often a power dynamic at play, even if only tacitly. Worse, if there is a *perception* of conflict or favoritism, this will impact other employees. This perception and impact exists because we've created a culture that goes against human nature, attempting to separate the professional world from the personal, separating the boardroom from the bedroom. Conflicts between people is an eternal problem that isn't going anywhere, and it's undoubtedly not simply solvable by written workplace policy. I would argue there are some situations where a relationship between a supervisor and subordinate or vendor and client, can be (and has been) conducted in a way that doesn't lead to bad circumstances. We don't have data to back up that statement because those often go unreported. Sex and power are inextricably linked, but that doesn't necessitate an unbalanced distribution of power in the way we normally think about it. If we employ empathy and emotional self-awareness, dollar to donuts these relationships will run a respectable course.

We need to embrace that love and sex and business and the workplace are co-existing, instead of resisting this notion. When we embrace and accept this, it stands to reason that we can more easily embody Sexual Intelligence in Business, into our daily practices. There is something that feels wrong with society, trying so hard to 'segment' and 'partition' off parts of our lives. I understand the urge to protect ourselves from those dire circumstances. I also fully understand some people have been and are currently in terrible harassment environments. But this is not the case for everyone 24/7. Moreover, I would argue that those toxic work and business environments would reduce significantly if Sexual Intelligence in Business was implemented. I would love to see a study published widely, and made broadly accessible to the general public, which contributes to the conversation around positive environments, and what makes those environments successful. The majority of the time, right now, things are decent, free from violence, or even, dare I say, good. I know some people don't want to hear that, out of fear, that advocates and leadership will take their foot off the gas and that people won't take seriously the issues women face if not promoted as ubiquitous and constant. And I get that, I really do. They are probably right. I wonder if there is a better way? Again, Sexual Intelligence in Business here might just do the trick. As humans, we are biologically programmed to build relationships; we are social creatures; we thrive in a community. Everything in business and work is relationship-based, I cannot stress this enough. We can and should be our beautiful selves, respectfully and lovingly. I'm not saying life is a bed of roses. As humans, we are full of conflict and drama, but life will hurt just a little bit less if we strive for a more positive viewpoint.

It should be no surprise that company culture has become a massive part of a successful business. Retaining good employees, it's the backbone of a happy and productive business and workplace. Without a positive culture, many employees will struggle to find the real value in their work, which leads to a variety of negative consequences for the company's bottom line. According to Deloitte's research in 2012, 94 percent of executives and 88 percent of employees believe a distinct culture is essential to a business's success. Alan Kholl writes in his 2018 Forbes article, "there is a strong correlation between employees who claim to feel happy and valued at work and those who say their company has a strong culture." Job satisfaction, employee wellness, meaning in their work, encouraging positivity, and fostering social connections are critical. It's all about people and relationships, and it always will be.

Business Affairs - the good kind ;)

One quick google and you are blasted with warnings. How to protect yourself. How things always end badly or what will make you susceptible to a workplace or business affair. It's like yelp reviews; most people write reviews because they are feeling bent and pissed off. These days, I doubt anyone would dare write an article promoting workplace affairs; and yet affairs in the workplace are the #1 place to engage in infidelity. There must be something enjoyable here happening. Also it is worth pointing out that workplace affairs and infidelity are not inextricably linked, you can have one without the other. There is much to be said about infidelity, whether its truly such a devilish, deceitful thing or is it a signal to us that they way we've structured monogamy may not be working for us so well. But that's for another book!

The affair's arc starts on a high, of course, and it's from the woman's point of view it always seems, in the writings I've read. They talk about how they knew the man was married and how they recognized it might get complicated, assuming all affairs are between a single, heterosexual cis-woman and a married man. Everything was hot and steamy and exciting, and then suddenly, the story jumps to, oh she can't get out of bed and is on antidepressants. Should this be taken as a cautionary example? Most definitely. But the issue that is ever-present in these subjects is we don't often hear about the opposite point of view. So we don't have a sense of how many times these things work out well. I think this skews the data and, more importantly, people's perceptions. I've spoken to a number of people about this. What I learned is that everything is not as dramatic as we've been led to believe.

More than 85 percent of affairs begin in the workplace. Considering how much time you spend with your spouse vs. the amount of time you spend with co-workers, this does not seem surprising. Day after day, you and your colleagues share the highs and lows, you bond over projects, tackle challenges together, and celebrate success. Naturally, this may lead to strong friendships and emotional attachments outside your marriage with close interactions. The workplace provides opportunities and proximity. And so it also makes good sense that with women's increasing entry into the workforce, we can see a correlation with a rise in the number of affairs. It's no wonder the workplace is the most common place affairs start. Guess what? There's nothing wrong with that! We need to free ourselves from the notion that the only place for sex is between a man and a woman, located in their marital bed. Moreover, if we open our minds towards new configurations other than the traditional, one man with one woman, in marriage, then perhaps we'd have less "affairs" and more "relationships", free of judgment.

But let's look at both sides of the coin. Indeed, there are consequences to having a workplace affair, beyond the fact that you may be deceiving a partner, but that's on you. You could be wasting value work time, thinking about the affair, or finding places to get together at the office, instead of focusing on productivity. At the same time, I believe all our relationships already take up a bit of mindshare during work; affairs aren't special here. We are also entitled to breaks. It is up to you how you want to spend them. Now, if you are being careless, using your work email for non-work-related messages (affairs or otherwise), maybe don't do that. Having sex at work or in places you risk getting caught, possibly avoid that too? Just sayin', there are other places to go; there's plenty of time to play in a 24 hour period. Be creative. The bottom line, just because you met at work doesn't mean you have the license to be non-productive. In fact, you can become more productive if you channel these hot and sexy feelings in the direction of work and business projects, as you will discover in other chapters.

Another consequence is that workplace affairs can affect employee morale if others are aware of it. I would recommend some self-monitoring and manage the relationship discreetly, otherwise you cause yourself some issues, maybe it's just not your jam. Now, if it's the type of affair that is not related to infidelity, meaning you are both single, but work together and don't want people to know, that's a bit of a different story. The problems with co-workers arise when, A) they feel like there's a secret amiss, or they are being deceived. That's never good. B) If you are messing around in offices while you should be working, well, that affects others because you should be working while you are at work. I know, crazy concept. Plus, you were hired to do a job, you should be performing that to the best of your ability and C) If you are involved with a superior, that will cause another set of problems, beyond power relations, it would be looked upon as favoritism (because it often times is, but not always) and that will bother your colleagues and may breed low morale, not to mention creating a hostile culture. More to the point, you should not actually get favoritism. It's not that other employees or the company care so much about you, although they might, but they do care much more about themselves and what benefits they get and don't get. This spells trouble.

Some work environments are very competitive and not the friendly work family they act like. Humans are self-interested and, unfortunately, may throw you under the bus if they feel the circumstance calls for it. In an ideal world, if you are just involved with a colleague, so long as you are productive and not too obvious, it's actually beyond me why people would ever get bothered. I'm sex-positive, so my perspective allows me to be happy for folks who are gettin' som'. Jealousy is a weird reaction sometimes, I'm delighted when I see others do well, get accolades or benefit. Sadly, we do not live in a perfect world, and although I firmly believe that many people have sound judgment, who can manage all this, not everyone does and as we can see by the types of cases that come forth and they types of scenarios that are studied, it is the poor judgements that get the press. At the same time, I have great hopes for humanity that we can get to a more beautiful and sex-positive place. But we're not there yet. So be mindful. Let's work on that together.

Then there's the worst consequence of all. Sexual harassment or sexual discrimination claims – If it's for real, obviously make a claim, both men and women. Please speak out, call out, take every measure possible to bring these horrible incidents to light. It's the only way we'll change behaviors. Humans fear punishment, usually. But if it's just that the breakup goes terrible, please deal with it like mature adults. Don't abuse the system just because you're mad or have hurt feelings. If you cannot manage your emotions and maintain positive and productive relations with everyone, then having an affair or workplace relationship is not for you. Understanding and accepting the consequences of your actions is the best course of action, in all cases, not just with sex and business.

CHAPTER 4

SECOND ORDER CONSEQUENCES OF #METOO

Second Order Consequences Of #metoo

When considering the #metoo movement, I invite you to put on your Sexual Intelligence lens, specifically looking at the principle of second-order consequences. There are also third and fourth and fifth, but for the purposes here, second is enough. What are second-order consequences, you ask? For every choice you make, there are consequences. First order consequences are relatively easy to evaluate and, in most cases, obvious. Also, in most cases, people stop there. But to make better choices and thoughtful decisions, one should go through the mental exercise of second and third-order consequences. This is important because, despite our intentions, there are interventions or consequences that come from the original that can cause harm. Can we predict the future? Of course not. But you would be surprised what we can anticipate and mitigate when we think past our initial assumptions. The worst part is we can destroy what our original intention was. This is an occurrence i've identified. Not as a result of the original #metoo by Burke, but from the social media twitter storms and what followed from that. In effect, the second order consequences can be considered in some ways, as a new level of an impediment to women's advancement in business.

A brief recount

#metoo was a movement born in 2006, when African American activist Tarana Burke began using the phrase "Me Too" on her social network to share her experience as a sexual harassment survivor. She invited other women of color who had been sexually abused to share their stories. Her sharing was far from the high-profile movement it is today, and Burke didn't intend "#metoo" to go viral but rather to raise awareness and provide a source of support that victims were not alone. It was more of a grassroots movement, says Burke, offering "empowerment through empathy." It began as a survivor-to-survivor sharing of stories amplifying the pervasiveness of sexual abuse, assault, exploitation, and harassment in underprivileged black communities.

The 2017 the hashtag #metoo movement began when American film executive Harvey Weinstein could no longer deny the scads of sexual harassment, abuse, or rape allegations of dozens of women. The New York Times published the first allegations on October 5, and within a week, Weinstein was fired from the company he had created. On October 15, Hollywood actress Alyssa Milano called-out on Twitter that anyone who has experienced sexual assault or harassment to reply to her tweet with the hashtag #metoo to expose the problem's scale. Half a million responded after just one day. After that, a profusion of additional high-profile harassment cases ensued.

The hashtag #metoo made headlines internationally, prompting women worldwide to share sexual assault or harassment experiences. Called a global watershed moment in the advancement of gender equality, #metoo offered a powerful platform to women in demonstrating the extent of sexual assault and harassment across society. In 2018, The New York Times reported that at least two hundred prominent men were fired after public allegations of sexual harassment, and women replaced half of those roles. I can't quite figure out if that is a good thing. Did companies place women there as a token? Probably some yes. Reasonable accommodation methods, there are mixed reviews about that. At the same time, only half of the men were replaced by women. Do we consider that low? Should it have been more? At least 920 women came forward, reports The New York Times, to say that one of these "prominent" men had subjected them to sexual misconduct. You may notice that these allegations are against high-profile men in the entertainment, the media, politics, and tech sectors. Many men deny any wrongdoing. Of course, everyone should get their day in court. But when we only hear about high profile cases, we don't get the full picture. It makes it hard to make decisions and draw conclusions. How representative are these high-profile cases?

And what's different for the millions of everyday people who shared and liked Tanara Burke's posts, and their own #metoo stories? Is it any better on the front lines of the workplace since 2017? How far down has the #metoo reached into the real-world, in the average work environment, where resources and support are as scarce as they are in the very communities outlined by Tanara Burke in the first #metoo?

#metoo has focused on internal interactions between colleagues or managers/subordinates, but those aren't the only situations where harassment can occur. Business interactions between different firms, clients, customers occur at conferences and trade shows, which bring individuals from a multitude of industries and sectors. These relationships, exchanges, and transactions are often conducted outside of office settings. Sexual harassment can occur anywhere that people are together.

What is sexual harassment? According to the Canada Department of Labour Code, this is "any conduct, comment, gesture, or contact of a sexual nature that is likely to cause offense or humiliation to any employee; or that might, on reasonable grounds, be perceived by that employee as placing a condition of a sexual nature on employment or any opportunity for training or promotion." It's detrimental; it ruins lives, can damage someone emotionally and professionally. In most modern legal contexts, sexual harassment is illegal. Canada's Labour Code "establishes an employee's right to employment free of sexual harassment and requires employers to take positive action to prevent sexual harassment in the workplace."

The unintended consequences of #metoo

Despite the ubiquitous awareness, significant progress, and the changes we see, unfortunately, the #metoo movement has also led to a few unintended consequences, a negative feedback loop, and a self-reinforcing problem not strategically dealt with will result in the opposite desired outcome. Somehow the #metoo movement has transformed into a narrative that if any detail is minutely challenged, an onslaught of anti-feminist accusations and fear-based mob tactics on social media ensues. Another unfortunate consequence is that we're mixing up misinterpretations or awkward behaviors, a misworded compliment, misinterpreted tone, undesired flirtation, misguided gestures, sex jokes (bad or funny), consensual affairs together with and in the same bucket as, sexual harassment and rape. These are not the same things. Further to that, the #metoo movement risks infantilizing women, assuming women don't have agency and need to be rescued and taken care of, which of course impedes progress towards equity in many arenas but specifically here, women's career advancement. The narrative around the movement seems to be focusing on the veneration of women and the denigration of men. If you are not a #metoo supported, you are automatically pro-sexual harassment, which could not be further from the truth.

Indeed, there is a perpetuating dilemma that all subjugated groups face when breaking out of their silence on important issues like racism, sexism, and discrimination. For the #metoo movement in particular, by categorizing women as victims, society gives them validation. Ok. You're victims. We've heard from you. We agree. You are victims. Now what? Has it turned the tables? Do women have the power now? They had it for a hot second. But how can we be sure this will result in long term change? The concerns that we have reinforced infantilizing women are real when most women rely on third party mechanisms to solve their problems. I know Margaret Atwood received a lot of backlash from her op-ed piece in The Globe and Mail, on January 13, 2018, but this passage really resonates:

Nor do I believe that women are children, incapable of agency or of making moral decisions. If they were, we're back to the 19th century, and women should not own property, have credit cards, have access to higher education, control their own reproduction or vote. There are powerful groups in North America pushing this agenda, but they are not usually considered feminists.

So how are women trying to deal with this? According to a Redbook magazine study, joint with Harvard Business Review on the issue of sexual harassment in the workplace, the most popular method for dealing with the abuse is to "ignore it, hoping it will stop." In life, there are certain things you can ignore; this isn't one of them. Sadly, only 14% of women ask a man to stop. Interestingly, they frame it as "ask," as if you need to do it politely? Shouldn't it be more like a demand, with consequences? How can women claim to deserve positions of power, and not be able to thwart comments, push back on harassment, say Fuck Off to unwanted advances? Now I know what some people may think, that women should not have to do that in the first place. Sure, there is some validity in that. But really, says who? Life isn't easy, and we are not as civilized as we'd like to think. Human beings are often self-serving who sometimes need some strong reactions to undesired behaviors. This is why we have laws and police to enforce them. Otherwise, we'd be living in a brutal chaotic society. It is imperative to keep moving towards growth, learn from our mistakes, become more enlightened, create a better world. At the same time, we cannot live in the 'land of the should be'.

Redbook also shares a story of a woman who continued to put up with inappropriate touching, patronizing comments, and more, and that she never reported it, hoping he would quit, fearing that if she said anything, she would be fired. She needed the job. This is an all too common scenario, but also she made incorrect assumptions. One day, she told him to fuck off and that "he was so shocked he literally never looked me in the eye again. "I felt like I did the right thing by standing up for myself," she says. And she did not get fired, not even close. So, what does that tell us? Say it upfront, the first time. Don't put up with this bs, and that perhaps some of that fear is in your head. *Limited beliefs* they call it. Take your agency.

Social Movements are not designed to last, and #metoo is no exception. The hard work of changing laws and policy is underway, despite the absence of flashy headlines and soundbites. We somehow need to tackle how to use the momentum towards positive systemic change, without causing fear and frenzy. Yes, you need to generate some shock and pain to get attention and hopefully affect people's behaviors. But how can women move from victim to vindicated? This is why I offer up the principles of Sexual Intelligence in Business. It's too easy to point to the government or the corporations for actions. Better to start with yourself.

#metoo has scared people and scared companies. What happens when companies get afraid? They write policy. Enter the HR Department! Unfortunately, most companies established and enforce their sexual harassment policies because a) if they don't, they lose massive credible risk public shaming, and b) avoid cases that go public, because that is very bad for business. And all of that fear-based decision making is hurting human interactions, and has the potential to reduce profitable business transactions, mentoring opportunities, and relationships for everyone in business and the workplace.

We have to change minds, not just behaviors. If the only reason men don't harass women is fear of punishment, the problem is not solved. And will continue to persist. No "company culture" will have a significant effect if men still *want* to misbehave/mistreat/violate women, even if their behavior is mitigated by punishment. Of course, it is absolutely necessary to put systems in place to, at a minimum, to attempt to prevent behaviors. But then the question is, why do some men have this in their minds in the first place? Whether they act on them or not, and regardless of *why* they act on them or not. I'm not talking about having sex in general, on their minds; research shows both men and women often think of sex, and close to the same frequency. But in terms of harassment and violence, is this a human nature problem? If yes, this doesn't explain why all men don't harass. If no, why do some men want to harass and for other men, it doesn't even cross their minds. Understanding this phenomenon will go a long way to eradicate harassment and violence. If there is something biological here, are we prepared to face a scenario where this is impossible to root out for some men?

To start, we need to ask, do men even know what sexual harassment is. In a study published in the Harvard Business Review, titled *Looking Ahead: How What We Know About Sexual Harassment Now Informs Us of the Future*, researchers wanted to understand if men and women had different impressions about what constitutes sexual harassment. There are claims that men were confused about what behaviors are considered sexual harassment or that women were "overly sensitive." The study evaluated nineteen behaviors and determined that most men and women know what it is. Atwater says, "The idea that men don't know their behavior is bad and that women are making a mountain out of a molehill is largely untrue. If anything, women are more lenient in defining harassment." We have to be careful here when studies talk about "most." We also need to consider that men may not be confused about what constitutes sexual harassment. Still, they are experiencing an identity crisis, as the masculine breadwinner construct is falling to pieces. We also need to realize that, in the straightforward cases, even the man denies it, the chances that women are over exaggerating is minimal, but in the behaviors mentioned above like misinterpretations or awkward behaviors, there is loads of room for subjectivity. Something else to point out if a woman likes the man and wants to or is dating him, some of those exact same behaviors may be desired and accepted. At the same time, it is interesting that the study considers women to be overly sensitive or not; instead of considering that it might not be an emotional response. Why do we continue to perpetuate that men would have a definitive *logical* misunderstanding of a definition, and women would have an *emotional* sensitivity? This is implicit bias at work here.

There can be grey areas between offense and humiliation regarding subjectivity and perceptions versus flirtation or genuine interest. It adds a layer of complexity that we are all dealing with. Just because a woman wears a sexy dress doesn't mean she deserves (or is asking) to get raped. The same applies upstream. There's a difference between sexual harassment and someone paying you a compliment or trying to plant a drunk kiss on you, commenting on how good you look today, and a full-on workplace love affair. All of these are different things and should be treated as such. There's a difference between rape, awkward flirting, touch on the elbow or words, and gestures caught in the web of sexual harassment. Realizing that some of the behaviors are unwanted, but do they need addressing using the same severity levels? Is awkward flirting or an unwanted compliment a slippery slope towards rape? I don't think so. I'm not suggesting, by any means, not to address situations, quite the opposite. The crime should suit the punishment, as they say.

The alternative isn't great either. If we leave it to HR to deal with, we can expect to see a deployment of new techniques aimed more at protecting companies than protecting employees. HR has these contracts or declarations, requiring employees who are dating to report to HR to sign paperwork affirming that they are willingly taking part in a consensual relationship, leading to yet another HR tactic to indemnify the company from the human impulses of its workers.

Men in the workplace are being very cautious when it comes to women. Lisa Kimmel, President and CEO of Edelman, tells the Financial Post that she's had conversations with "a number of senior male business leaders in Canada," who told her they were shying away from providing mentorship to female subordinates "out of fear of what might potentially happen" and to "reduce their risk profile to zero...

and the movement will ultimately hurt – not help – women in the long run."

Again, the study *Looking Ahead: How What We Know About Sexual Harassment Now Informs Us of the Future,* Atwater found that following the #metoo movement, men are significantly more reluctant to interact with their female colleagues. A few statistics from that study show that 57% of men avoid one-on-one meetings with female co-workers, 44% of men are more likely to exclude women from social interactions, and 16% of men would be hesitant to hire an attractive woman. It wasn't the intention, but the #metoo movement doesn't seem to be bridging any gaps here.

In another article from Bloomberg, titled *Wall Street Rule for the #metoo Era: Avoid Women at All Cost* by Gillian Tan and Katia Porzecanski, talk about just how far these HR policies are willing to go. No more dinners with female colleagues. Don't sit next to them on flights. Book hotel rooms on different floors. Avoid one-on-one meetings. Just hiring a woman these days is risky business, because what if she took something he said the wrong way? Because it only takes once...

Such positioning isn't uncommon. If you're American Vice-President Mike Pence, you even get to make up a policy. The Mike Pence rule stipulates that he will not dine alone with a woman, and if there is an event with alcohol involved, his wife must be present. She's a lawyer by the way. The "Rule" also implies that there should be chaperons at business meetings, having meetings in rooms only with glass walls, keeping distance in elevators. One on one time is critical for career advancement because networking, relationships, and mentorship are everything. These Pense Rules make it impossible to build relationships; Business or otherwise. There are personal and professional implications; no promotion, no mentorship, no advancement, no camaraderie, and no chance of building friendships or more. Women are locked out. Is this overkill? Totally. This is the epitome of second-order consequences. But people are acting very extreme in all directions these days. As former Toronto Star business reporter Tara Deschamps states in a 2018 Canadian Press Article, "Holiday parties were a huge issue too, and of course, business travel is big as well because often you are sitting side-by-side 12 to 16 hours a day and you are not just working together, you are eating together, you are staying at the same hotel, consuming alcohol, entertaining clients, it can make for a very intimate scenario." But that's the point. Time spent together builds relationships, which most of the time, works out well.

To understand better the differences between flirtation and sexual harassment, one must become attuned to social cues. Here again the framework of Sexual Intelligence in Business can be helpful. We must also consider that there is a bit of subjectivity here. We also have to consider the sheer amount of differences in culture, religion, upbringing, there is so much room for misinterpretation. Not every word or gesture can be written into law or policy, and so understanding that it's not just about what you think constitutes flirtation or sexual harassment, but also what the other person perceives or intends. Is the person smiling at you in genuine, shiny eyes, raised eyebrows kind of way, or are they smiling at you in an uncomfortable, gawky, looking you up and down sort of way? Are they outward and obvious in their reception to your advance? Did you determine some type of consent, verbal or otherwise? What indicators did you use? Has the person already declined you in any way or degree? Do you find yourself trying to convince? Do you know the difference between playing hard to get and someone who wants you to stop? Have you rejected someone respectfully? Are you sure they have well understood you? These are a bunch of questions we can ask ourselves and others, to be more sure.

As you can see, these are situations that are so nuanced; you can barely even ask any of these questions without there being some degree of ambiguity. So if you cannot read a cue and are not entirely confident, you better go straightforward. Have you paid a compliment to only a sexually defined body part, or are you complimenting the person themself? What is the context of the situation? Is this a job interview? If you do not have people-reading skills and are too afraid to ask things outright, then what can we do? This is problematic, because many are doing just that, and "checking out" completely. All of this required some level of bravery, always has, even before #metoo. Men have experienced the brunt of massive rejection; perhaps that is why they turned it into a pure numbers game instead of being more observant. They cast a wide net. Everyone's role here is to observe and proceed respectably, which will get everyone the results they seek. It does require effort on everyone's part. If you are uncomfortable, it is your responsibility to speak up; the first time should be respectful. Give people a chance. There is a deep need for empathy, for everyone to understand there is a difference between flirtation and sexual harassment and it may take time to teach everyone this.

Another unintended consequence of the #metoo movement is that it does not speak for all feminists or women. Camile Paglia, who considers herself an extreme feminist, writes from her book Free Women, Free Men, Sex Gender Feminism, "When men step out of line women should deal with it on the spot. Most men are cowed by women! Any woman worth her salt should know how to deal with men and put them in their place. Women must demand respect, and over time, they will get it. It is foolish to think that substantial change in human psychology and sexual relationships can be changed through legislation and regulation, that is, through authoritarian intrusion into private life". It is a very different point of view from what we could call mainstream feminists. Although I don't agree with her entirely, there's some good stuff in there. We can see how this plays out more in business and the workplace, due to power dynamics with the eternal nature versus culture debate that she postulates. The creation of culture and society is our way of tampering, dealing with, and organizing our chaotic, animalistic natures. We need to find a way to balance this. Don't forget, sex is primal, not a political nicety.

The current situation around the #metoo narrative is controlled to the point that it's hard to have a conversation around it, to discuss anything that may call certain things into question. Each harassment case is not evaluated on its own, but considered evidence towards supporting the movement itself. There is no innocence until proven guilty, nor is there justice for victims; the cases are merely cogs in the #metoo machine of righteousness. Because even though historically, women and victims of sexual harassment have, for far too long, not been believed, and it has often taken several pile on cases to get justice served. At the same time, now the cases are being venerated in a way that constructs a male profile, that all men are indeed participating in, or have a propensity towards, sexual harassment, which is terrible and false. Because if we are going to be objective, In all cases, that means there are not "types" of men that are sexual harassers or rapists, just as there are no "types" of women who get sexually harassed or raped. Or is there? Is that what the #metoo supporters are trying to say?

Another problem is women are no more ethical than men, and some women have taken advantage of the #metoo movement as a method to usurp power. As Margaret Atwood points out, *"My fundamental position is that women are human beings, with the full range of saintly and demonic behaviours this entails, including criminal ones. They're not angels, incapable of wrongdoing. If they were, we wouldn't need a legal system."* It demonstrates that we need to be cautious about dealing with accusers and the accused; each case should be looked at distinctly. Simultaneously, we may need a different system for sexual harassment, violence, and rape cases. I don't know what that looks like, but it seems to me that what we have is not working too well.

As demonstrated above, there are numerous second-order consequences that came out of the #metoo movement, that certainly were not intentional. But here they are. They are real. We need to address them. Applying the Sexual Intelligence in Business framework is a good first step in tackling these issues, at least from an individual standpoint. The only person you can really change in the world, is yourself.

We need to expand the narrative of the #metoo movement and I hope this book provokes more conversations. I have enormous amounts of hope and idealism for humanity, but I also know that humans are not perfect creatures. We are driven by greed and fear almost as much as we are motivated by love and sex. If you are in an uncomfortable situation, speak out, leave, quit, press charges. Do something, anything but silence. Empowerment is not magically bestowed, sprinkled over like fairy dust when laws become ratified, and policies are in place. It's something you enact, yourself. Now. Today. That's real empowerment.

CHAPTER 5
POWER, PATRIARCHY AND PERCEPTION

Power, Patriarchy And Perception

There are many types of power in this world, but the only thing that matters in business is who holds it. The answer in 2020 is simple: men. Of course, historically, they had to be the power player. They were put in the role of family caretakers; they were the hunters, breadwinners, kings, and ran the farm and family business. Over the years, the number of women in management and c-suite positions has, by all means, increased. Thirty-seven of the Fortune 500 companies and 10 percent of heads of states are now women. In reality, a paltry sum when you think that women make up half of the world's population. But even that paltry sum, those thirty seven women, seem to scare the other half.

The problem is people don't give up power easily once they've had a taste of it. Since women have stepped into the office next to their male counterparts, some men seem to feel threatened; they have resorted to sexual harassment and other more subtle forms of sabotage. Sexual harassment is not about sex. It's about power. In the office, it's a power grab, an attempt to dominate. The idea of attaining power is so heady it makes us forget our good sense and do things we know we shouldn't. It's a cheap card to play but one that was tolerated simply because of the range of acceptable behavior offered to men.

Various research studies have demonstrated that many gender differences occur by manipulating people's sense of power. When it comes to power, there is a specific range of acceptable behaviors one can exhibit when they have different power levels. Obviously, and usually, when one has full control (what does that mean exactly?) but when one does, one may exhibit (and get away with) a more comprehensive range of behaviors, both positive and negative. When it is determined that one has less power, stepping outside of power (whether that's aggressive, weakness, etc.), one is punished regardless of levels. When we say punished, that could mean a range of outcomes from public shaming, direct conflict, job/opportunity loss, or criminal charges. The range of acceptable behaviors is a moving target, and always changing, by time and by context. #metoo was supposed to change the scope of acceptable behavior for men and also women. But did it really?

Before answering this question, we first have to consider the range of acceptable behavior and attitude that women in business have encountered since they stepped into the boardroom. Ronit Kark et al., in How Women Manage the Gendered Norms of Leadership, 2018, calls this a Gender Bind: "Women, face the need to be warm and nice (what society traditionally expects from women), as well as competent or tough (what society traditionally expects from men and leaders). The problem is that these qualities are seen as opposites creating a "catch-22" and "double bind" for women leaders." Women leaders are seen to be confident or likeable, but rarely both.

Anne Wilson Schaef, an American clinical psychologist and author points out in her 1992 book, Women's Reality: An Emerging Female System, men make up the dominant culture. "Women are motivated to understand and know a man's way of being, while men don't need to make an effort to understand a woman's way of seeing and experiencing the world." As an example, look at the coverage of 2016 American presidential candidate Hilary Clinton. She suffered attacks on her female characteristics, ridiculed for not being sensitive and touchy-feely enough to being called a witch, a power-hungry demon, a lesbian, a liar. She had her sanity attacked with accusations that she had brain damage after a concussion. And, what she wore, was a topic never subjected to male candidates. I'm not sure I have seen this level of base attack on any previous presidential candidate. Do you think that was a coincidence? Certainly not. Desperate times call for desperate measures. Is it any surprise these were the chosen attacks? It seems the strategy is not to criticize Hilary as a candidate, but to criticize Hilary for being a woman.

Enter the post #metoo era, where women were supposed to level out the playing field finally. Those who were victimized by sexual harassment, most likely not realizing it, we're speaking out to reclaim their power and heighten their range of acceptable behavior. Their range of behavior before was to shut their mouths and accept the inequalities and harassment they were facing. Through #metoo, they spoke out loud. Many women benefited from this, not just the promoted women but also feminists, activists, promoters of #metoo; they all gained notoriety.

Unfortunately, wearing the victim as a badge of honour has in some ways led to less power, more towards infantilizing women, that requires them to be watched and monitored by men for their protection, and in turn, a loss of power.

How you might ask, by creating space for women to stand up for themselves and that some powerful men are being called out for their actions, does that equate to a loss of power for women? Simple. HR policies. The men in charge of companies fearing lawsuits and damaging campaigns, mandated their HR departments to come up with stiff policies to negate any chance of a worker slipping through the cracks and saying the big man in charge doesn't care about women's rights. Prior to #metoo, many companies and organizations had some form of policy regarding personal/sexual relationships already on the books. Some had declaration forms to fill out. Other companies simply wanted employees to declare them to their managers verbally. Then after #metoo, policy went craaaaaazyzzzyyy!

Indeed, I have witnessed and been subjected to the changes that have resulted from the #metoo movement—having my relationships and sexual expression controlled by the workplace sexual harassment policy does not sit well with me. It's an infringement of liberty and choice. Moreover, it's ripe for abuse.

If women's goal is to obtain more power and a broader range of acceptable behavior, should we be limiting our liberties and choices? Is HR, in reality, servicing the male agenda instead of protecting women?

For the longest time, different levels of institutions controlled the discourse, and thereby framework of power and sex and in what ways we could talk about it. So who gets to decide what kind of sex is acceptable/good (and under what condition), who are the sluts/pimps/perverts? Hence, it's about power. Again, Oscar Wilde said "Everything in the world is about sex except sex. Sex is about power." One could infer from this, that people hide behind institutions, that are setup and centered around both the proliferation of sex, the prevention of unsanctioned sex and how much time (and labour wages) we spend on sex.

With the commencement of industrialization, any time or energy on purely pleasurable activities was strongly frowned upon. Authorities doubled down on the sanctity of marriage, to the point that, sex outside the confines of marriage is not simply prohibited, but repressed, made unspeakable and unthinkable. Freud was effective in opening discussions on sexuality, and thereby, the discourse had transferred to the academic, medical and confessional realm of psychiatry. There is a theory called the repressive hypothesis that suggests a paradox that speaking about sex is both rebellious and is instrumental to our personal liberation. Foucault asks, how can we claim that we can't talk about sex and at the same time talking so much about it. We claim its taboo and yet it's everywhere, movies, music, advertising, it's everywhere!

To Foucault, discourse is very important. If you think about it, language and knowledge are closely linked to power. Who decides what gets said, holds the power, hence the saying, "knowledge is power". One who determines what can be talked about also decides what can be known. When you control knowledge and public narratives, you control how people think and how people behave and who people become. How does this relate to Sexual Intelligence in Business? We have become prevented from talking about sex in business and at work, for two opposing reasons. To speak freely about sex, to enjoy sex, or public display of sexuality, is to invite sexual harassment. Sex and sexual harassment by extension, is distracting from work and productivity. This costs companies money, labour, and reputation. Further to that, to criticize #metoo is equated to being anti-feminist and pro-patriarchy and women's sexual pleasure is relegated to a non-priority as pay equity and c-suite positions are top of mind. Given all that, I would argue that we can still apply the Sexual Intelligence framework in business and the workplace as the principles tuck neatly in between these opposing binary conundrums. With respect, empathy, reading emotional and body cues, ensuring the other's needs are heard and met, maintaining a positive attitude, keeping emotions under control during education and conversations that are difficult.

Instead of sex being something we can also have fun with, and pursue with reckless passion, it has been converted into a topic we must approach with restraint. Sex is increasingly an object of knowledge, as we academize the study and research, and shift it towards the medical domain. Sex has become an important target of study, governments are increasingly interested in the vital statistics of their populations to be understood and classified, only to be talked about in a certain, sanctioned manner. Again, Foucault connects this deepening of discourse directly to the exercise of power.

Foucault describes this relationship between pleasure and power as a spiral: they pursue one another in a circular pattern, power seeking pleasure and pleasure drawn to power. The powers of analysis we have directed toward perverse sexuality have not acted to repress it but to help it flourish.

The only way we can balance power in business and work, is by redetermining the dominion of our knowledge, discourse and expression of sex. Until we can embrace and own our sexualness, in a respectful, confident, way until we own our bodies, women will continue to relinquish power. This counts for all genders. Sex is ubiquitous, we need to get comfortable with that, in all environments. It's the pink elephant in the room.

Lastly, it is my estimation that there is actually an unlimited amount of power and that it is not distributed in the way that people currently imagine. One of the ways that men manifested power, historically, was through physical violence. The fact is, men on average tend to have more physical power. But we can see that, in western societies, with the rule of law, men physically abusing women has reduced. It's not as easy as it once was, to threaten women with violence. Not entirely unfortunately, and certainly not globally. The point is that this form of power is slipping. Then the power shifted towards economics, access to money, access to resources. Now I would also argue that women have access to very powerful resources themselves, but have been reluctant to use them when necessary. More to come on that in future chapters. But one only needs to look towards economic crisis, global pandemics, not to cause, but to shine light on how fragile those systems really are. Think about different prominent figures like comedians, radio show hosts, etc, one slip of the tongue, one false word, and their career is over. Think about a company that does a faux pas in business, it catches on social media and this affects a company's bottom line. The power of consumers, the power of customers, the power of globalization and social media, has in fact, highlighted that power is actually a construct, its fleeting, and it's a perception. What that means for everyone, is that it is gettable. It is much more accessible than originally imagined and I would argue, it's at your fingertips. Indeed, power in the form of high level positions and decision making, remains a barrier, but things are changing. It is not a zero sum game, which hopefully should relieve some of the fears that men are facing. In relation to the type of power that comes from within, this is accessible, it's infinite, there's enough for everyone. Sexual Intelligence is one of the keys to unlocking this.

Patriarchy

Patriarchy is defined in the dictionary as a system of society or government in which the father or eldest male is head of the family, and descent is traced through the male line. In many cultures, men are more likely to hold economic, cultural and political power and earn the most significant salaries.

With movements like #metoo and more people expressing dissatisfaction with the status quo, the gender equity movement finally seems to be winning the argument. Of course, #metoo expedited that process. To win the game, we need to ask why the Patriarchy exists, and why does it persist?

Most explanations are political, social or economic. However, some are examining these questions from a scientific perspective – especially the evolutionary origins of inequality and gender, sex and power. Authors of the book Why Does Patriarchy Persist?,

Carol Gilligan and Naomi Snider, write about the connection between Patriarchy's persistence to the psychology of loss. Gilligan and Snider start with a simple premise. "We live in a relationship with one another; the idea of an isolated individual standing alone is absurd. Our actions affect the people we love and care about, family, friends, etc., so we have to be aware of those relationships. But Patriarchy is a culture based on a gender binary and hierarchy that forces a split between a self and relationships. In effect, men have selves whereas women are ideally selfless; they have relationships which surreptitiously serve men's needs."

The importance of the self for feminism is reflected in Simone de Beauvoir's The Second Sex: Woman as Other in 1949 in her provocative declaration, "He is the Subject, he is the Absolute—she is the Other." It's a statement that elevates all men over women, but it also shows that women come to experience themselves as others, a non-person, and non-selves. But if you have no self, you are not in a relationship. The authors' thesis points to a paradox: we give up relations to have "relationships."

In part, Patriarchy persists because of its psychological function as a defence against loss. In this sense, "Patriarchy is at once a source of lost connection and a defence against further loss. A source of trauma and defence against trauma." The persistence of Patriarchy is premised on women's compliance and silence. By being silent, women can't build off or share cultural experiences. They don't grow, and they don't learn from one another. "Our combined silence becomes complicit in allowing patriarchy to remain the status quo."

As a culture, Patriarchy exists as a set of rules and values that specify how men and women should act in order to be protected. There are consequences to breaking those rules. Imaging how we are living in cities, in much greater numbers together, and exposed to more people. This facilitates our ability to communicate our feelings and to pick up others' feelings that threatens the structures of hierarchy. "By resisting pressures to disengage ourselves, from our honest voices," writes Carol Gilligan in Joining the Resistance in 2011, "We become able to open the way for the development of a more humane way of thinking about personal and political relationships. Feelings of empathy and compassion for another's suffering, or humanity make it difficult to maintain or justify inequality." On the other side, there is a human inclination to keep things as they are. Often times women buy into the benevolent sexism, because it's easier. Change is hard, and people prefer consistency.

Although not originally intended as such, patriarchy became a system of control and submission that seems to have resulted from patrilineage being essential and currency of exchange. The process is instituted and taught, passed down generation to generation, to both girls and boys. As Bell Hooks says, "Learning to wear a mask is the first lesson in patriarchal masculinity that a boy learns. He learns that his core feelings cannot be expressed if they do not conform to sexism's acceptable behaviors as male. Boys are asked to give up the true self to realize the patriarchal ideal; boys learn self-betrayal early and are rewarded for these acts of soul murder." (bell hooks, The Will to Change: Men, Masculinity, and Love.) On the opposite side, women learn explicitly to be submissive concerning others, robbed of freedom, liberty and power.

There is much talk about destroying or smashing Patriarchy, but there's no comprehensive system replacing it. Social systems are not easily destroyed and replaced in a world and society that loves to classify and categorize. 'Better the devil you know' attitude is what holds us all back from systemic change. It's not for lack of desire; it's for lack of something mostly tangible. The sum is more significant than its parts. So we can break things down into incremental steps, as we are doing. Women vote. Gay rights. Women's equity, Black Lives Matter. But we still cannot "imagine" a new system. We have to name it. Describe it, and then people will subscribe. Humanarchy? Sapianarchy? Genearchy? Progenarchy? Civilarchy? Just throwing those out there...

Sexism

Many of us believe to know what sexism is, a prejudice about a group of people, founded in conceptualizations of one gender as superior or having higher status than another gender in a particular domain, leading to discrimination. But allow me to tell you about a few sub-components of the definition that are quite interesting. You may recognize them play out in your daily lives.

Ambivalent Sexism

A framework composed of "hostile sexism" and "benevolent sexism." The word "ambivalent" is used to describe sexism's analysis because this type of bias includes both negative and positive evaluations of women.
Glick and Friske in 1997 write that,

- Hostile sexism consists of overtly negative evaluations and stereotypes about gender, such as the idea that women are incompetent and inferior to men.
- Benevolent Sexism (way worse!) represents appraisals that may appear subjectively positive (subjective to the person who is evaluating), but are damaging, for example, the idea that women need to be protected by men

The theory has primarily been developed by social psychologists Peter Glick and Susan Fiske.

Sexism perpetuates patriarchal structures and reinforces prescribed gender roles and consists of hostility toward women, performed by men. Here's the perplexing part, both women and men can (and often do) endorse sexist beliefs about each other and themselves. In other words, women can also express sexist attitudes about men or women. Has anyone ever heard of "mean girls"? Women can be worse to other women. I maintain, rigid gender roles can damage women and men.

Glick and Fiske in 1996 asserted that hostile and benevolent sexism reinforce each other in a complimentary way. Preserving traditional gender roles and conserving patriarchal structures of women as subordinate. Both Benevolent and Hostile sexism share the assumption that women are inferior and restrict women to a lower social status. So what is hostile sexism? It reflects misogyny (hatred of women by men). It's expressed through deliberate negative evaluations of women, such as, but not limited to, women's beliefs as incompetent, unintelligent, emotional, and sexually manipulative (uh oh!). Benevolent sexism reflects evaluations of seemingly positive women. Examples are attitudes that include the veneration of women in wife, mother, and child caretaker roles (the love of a mother as greater than the love of a father, or how women are more caring), the romanticizing of women as objects of heterosexual affection (women are beautiful, opening car doors) , and the belief that men must protect women.

While benevolent sexism may not seem to be harmful to women on the surface, these beliefs are incredibly problematic to gender equity and restrict women's personal, professional, political, and social opportunities. Because benevolently sexist attitudes appear favorable, people often don't identify these beliefs as a form of gender-based prejudice. Furthermore, benevolent sexism reinforces the status quo, manifested in chivalry, which oddly, some individuals may find comforting. I can open my door, carry my box and move my damn fridge; thank you very much. Here's the kicker, people may find it difficult to distinguish between kindness, tradition, and benevolent sexism.

Furthermore, women may be inadvertently perpetuating sexist beliefs about women. There is a tricky balance of power between men and women. Men may tend to have structural power, but women tend to have dyadic power. Dyadic power consists of the notion that men depend on women to fulfill specific goals, such as heterosexual intimacy and childbearing. Glick and Fiske continued to study the phenomenon and in 2001 asserted that men's dependence on women fuels benevolently sexist attitudes, leading to idolization and the placing of women on a pedestal.

One can see how power dynamics, a patriarchal system and sexist attitudes both inhibit and reinforce. The lesson to be learned here is that although Patriarchy is systemic, you don't need to wait until the crushing fall occurs before you change your behavior, especially if it just comes down to definitions. When it comes to dynamics and attitudes, and again I'm going to repeat myself a million times here, using the principles of Sexual Intelligence in Business, gaining knowledge and self-awareness while shifting your mindset and attitude, is a practical starting point to change all that for yourself.

CHAPTER 6
THE FREEDOM TO NEGOTIATE

The Freedom To Negotiate

When it comes to negotiation, most people wing it. Those who negotiate often have the experience and advantage of making mistakes in the past and honing their skills over time. There is a real art to effective negotiation, some techniques seem just to come out organically, a bit hard to write out step by step, never mind instruct and teach someone. It can feel like either you have it or you do not. Fortunately for you, there are a few approaches based on research or special techniques to explore here and many authors and experts to learn from.

Understanding here this chapter (and most of the book) is referring to cis-gender, assumptions of heterosexuality, and from a western viewpoint. Mostly because that is what is contained in the research. Outlining all configurations could make for an entirely new and super relevant book, one that I may write next. What can be gleaned are some insights that can be mapped onto any relationship with a power difference.

Negotiation, on the whole, has a bit of a bad reputation. Many people fear negotiating the same way they fear the dentist or public speaking. Effective negotiation is viewed as a nasty or an aggressive endeavor, where two sides argue, debate, bully, and sometimes screw people over. The reason why negotiation has that reputation is that it does sometimes go down like that. This may be why women tend to steer clear. However, we are actually regularly negotiating throughout the day. Nearly every human interaction is a negotiation of some kind. So it's probably in everyone's best interest if we call get good at it.

Now, there's a whole world of academic research (and business expert writing) surrounding how people negotiate, in business and in life. Again, we are indeed constantly negotiating. At the same time, there are equal amounts of variation and often contrasting opinions and techniques. The beauty of that is you can discover and employ the methods you are comfortable with to get the results you are seeking.

Interestingly, much of the research split men's and women's techniques and attaches them to socially constructed gender characteristics. Whereas the books of experts tend to give straight-up approaches, the "how-to", in this chapter, we can look at the spectrum of thought and how sex intertwines with that. Whether people want to admit it, sex is present in negotiations. We can look at it from a gender perspective, from a power relations perspective, from a sexual perspective. Negotiating in the bedroom is very similar to negotiating in the boardroom. People find negotiating in the bedroom equally if not more challenging than in business, but many of the same principles apply. This chapter is not designed to help us negotiate better in the bedroom per se, but the techniques can be applied in both locations. All locations.

Both in the bedroom and the boardroom, the most important point to realize is that we have the liberty to negotiate. We may or may not come out of the negotiation with exactly what we want all the time, but if we apply the negotiation techniques in this chapter, we can drastically increase our chances of getting most of what we want, at least getting more than we had going in. We have to ask for what we want. If we intermix the principles of Sexual Intelligence in Business, this will raise our game, optimize results and maximize outcomes.

There is reason to believe that flirting and negotiation can result in positive outcomes. A study in 2012 at U.C. Berkeley, conducted by Professor Laura Kray, Professor Connsen Locke et. al, called "Feminine Charm: An Experimental Analysis of its Costs and Benefits in Negotiations" published in the Journal of Personality and Social Psychology Bulletin, concluded that sometimes, under certain conditions, when women are negotiating with men, they might fare better in their negotiation if they (the woman) flirt. "It's flirtation that generates positive results," says Professor Laura Kray, and that flirtation "is not overt sexual advances but authentic, engaging behavior without serious intent." The study found that "female flirtation signals attractive qualities such as confidence, which is considered essential to successful negotiators."

In contrast, there are concerns that flirtation, or any display of sexual expression by women, will not only have adverse effects but devalues women. One could conclude that this may erase the advances women have made thus far. Paula Gutlove, Professor of Practice in Negotiation & Conflict Management, Simmons School of Management, comments that after the release of Kray's article, the media headlines promoted women's flirtation to negotiate better deals. "The stories touted flirting as the new, secret ingredient that should work for all women. The headlines titillate, sex sells, and so, apparently, does devaluing women." Many negotiation experts have a few strategies to be a great negotiator, including building rapport and trust, and respect. Dr. Gutlove discourages women from flirting as a negotiation tactic because there are ethical implications. She argues that flirting devalues women and alludes that no woman can both flirt and maintain respect. Of course, not only do I think we can flirt and maintain respect, I think it gives everyone an advantage. What's more, if flirting devalues women, then it stands to reason that all women should stop flirting in all cases, not just in business. Why would men only devalue women in business and not the personal arena as well? The message this sends is that all women must cover up everything feminine, sexual, flirty, anything remotely enticing because men can't control themselves and if they ever hope to gain respect by any person, then women must act like men. This says that sex is not respectable. And if men can't control themselves, then who's really in control here? You teach people how to treat you, and so if you think that flirting devalues you, that is what you'll project. If you believe you have value regardless, you will project that as well.

Professor Gutlove continues to cite former Secretary of State Madeleine Albright as an example. In the past, Albright admits to using her feminine charm in bilateral negotiations with foreign heads of state, and many credit her as an excellent negotiator and equally charming. Are we saying it's acceptable for Madeleine Albright to use her charm because she is not a supermodel (not judging whether she is or isn't, these are the assumptions), and we believe nothing will ultimately come of it anyway? Whereas, if statistically speaking, by society's definition, a sexy and beautiful woman did use feminine charm in negotiations, it would be wrong? If people identify you as a threat or are jealous, they will find things to try and bring you down. How dare she be smart and beautiful, and use those qualities! We don't do this to men, why do we do this to women? Remember the Hilary Clinton example...

Lastly, Gutlove states that "Competent, talented women should not ignore their value and flatter their negotiating partner with sexual innuendos to be considered likeable to get the job done. Not only does such behavior demean women, putting them in a subservient position, but it doesn't gain the woman any value at the bargaining table." The problem with this statement is that Gutlove makes the grand assumption that all flirting and flattery is a direct line to intercourse, that if I flirt with you, I'm giving you the signal that I'm promising to sleep with you one day. That's quite a leap! Moreover, she assumes that women flirt because they want to be considered likable instead of realizing that it is a useful tool and aids in relationship building. She also presumes that women don't like flirting and use it as a necessary evil. I disagree.

It is also interesting that the term flirting is often associated with women, and the term charming is associated with men. You can see how sex gets implicated in women, whereas the power of influence is associated with the men. From my perspective, it's a matter of semantics. It's like calling the man ambitious but the women aggressive, for the same behaviors. It's common for people to choose their terminology based on whether they want to reward or punish identical actions. The key here for women is not to eliminate the behavior to win a war on semantics. Instead, own the behavior. Take it back, on your terms. Another two words that are subtly the same and different, manipulation and influence. Men have long thought that women use their "powers of sexuality" and "femininity" to manipulate men. Besides the fact that flirting comes very natural and comfortable for me, I want to use all the tools in my toolbox to influence people towards my goals. It's about intent. Using your powers for evil is manipulation. Using your powers for good is influence.

How does one measure what is flirting and what is not? Flirting is subjective, and some of us are flirty by nature, in a friendly way, but I don't feel disrespected or devalued. I do pretty well at the negotiation table. I think there's a lot of room between smiling, being charming, being flirtatious, outright sexual innuendoes, and offering sex outright. I also wonder if anyone has asked men if they realize when someone is flirting with them? Do they even care? Does it influence their decision? If you look at some of the research, they make men sound so damn scrupulous. If getting the deal done means ignoring a woman's flirting, I'm pretty sure they will do that. At the same time, there's research that suggests that looks matter. There's even more evidence that demonstrates that relationships matter. If being flirty or charming, from a man or a woman, helps build those bonds, it seems that it might be worth trying. We get the sense that it is acceptable that men use their charm. Nobody seems too worried about devaluing men or losing respect for men if they are charming and flirty. Yet, we keep holding women to different standards. And when I say "we," I mean everyone. When we keep acting out the roles, in a way, we perpetuate them.

Again, in 2012, Dr. Laura Kray and her associates wrote that the definitions of friendliness and flirtatiousness are very close to collaborative negotiating. In *Feminine Charm: An Experimental Analysis of its Costs and Benefits in Negotiations,* published in Personality and Social Psychology Bulletin, that this is a "win/win style" when at least one of the parties is empathic to the other parties and tries to grow the value of the overall negotiation. Kray et al. suggest that you should be friendly, be yourself, be empathetic towards the other person, but don't lose sight that you are negotiating for yourself. Call it flirting. Call it collaborative negotiating. Call it what you will, but if the other party doesn't believe you are looking out for yourself, they will win the negotiation. "Women are uniquely confronted with a tradeoff in terms of being perceived as strong versus warm. Using feminine charm in negotiation is a technique that combines both," said Kray.

We can conclude that flirtation generates positive results for those comfortable with the method, signalling attractive qualities such as confidence, which is considered essential to successful negotiators. Kray said many of her students who are senior women executives admit they love to flirt and describe themselves as "big flirts." Kray maintains flirting is not unprofessional if it remains playful and friendly, "the key is to flirt with your natural personality in mind." The most useful quality one can have these days is understanding people and situations to employ the best strategies and approaches to lead to all parties' best results.

Negotiating Salary

According to Harvard Business Review in 2018, "research suggests that 20 percent of women never negotiate their salary offer. When women choose not to negotiate a starting salary, you risk leaving money on the table, to the tune of ~$7,000 the first year, and possibly between $650,000 and $1 million throughout a 45+year career." Why are women reluctant to negotiate? Women find negotiating uncomfortable and fear they will come off ungrateful for the opportunity and the offer may be rescinded.

Much of the negotiation advice and research surrounds compliance and agreement with socialized gender norms that associate certain qualities and characteristics to men and women. Besides, research and advice about women's negotiation usually point to men's negative parts instead of the positive ones. A good woman is defined as helpful, modest, kind, and focused on her family/community rather than her self-interest. Meanwhile, the ideal man is direct, assertive, competitive, and ambitious. In her 2019 New York Times writer, Joan C Williams writes that "This version of masculinity maps perfectly onto what we expect from leaders, in business and politics. Women in leadership need to display these "masculine" qualities, but they risk being seen as bad women and bad people when they do. So savvy women learn that they must often do a masculine thing (which establishes their competence) in a feminine way (to defuse backlash)."

Other research finds that women make similar accommodations while negotiating. Williams says that "what women need to do to survive and thrive in the world is exactly the opposite of what they need to do to change it." But you can't win em' all. This Likeability Trap is something women need to get over. You have to be okay with not being liked. Stereotypes and discriminations still exist, but we have to be careful not to keep perpetuating these ourselves. For sure men want to be liked too, everyone does. But they are not going to compromise a negotiation over it, and women should not either.

After reading from several sources, I've amalgamated a few tips to more effective negotiations. This is not exhaustive, but it's a good start.

To Start

You'll need to assess whether employing small talk at the beginning of a negotiation to develop a relationship before or get down to business. You need to spend some time understanding who you are negotiating with, so you can get a read on them and what they want. Being able to give the 'other side' as much of what they want, will help you get what you want. Ask lots of questions, listen very carefully.

Tip:

Know your audience. Adjust accordingly. Say less, listen more.

Mindset

Because of socialization, women tend to identify negotiating as a chore and they would prefer to avoid it. Whereas men tend to see negotiating as a game or a challenge. Men are seen as being more competitive than women, although I'm sure female athletes will take offense to that! Men may be more focused on winning than a woman in some cases, but not all and that can change.

Tip:

Enter a negotiation ready for a challenge, no matter what. There will be back and forth. You want to approach the negotiation on a level playing field with the other person and this will help you reach your goals.

Confidence

Until you have undertaken many, many negotiations and get comfortable with the strategies, your confidence might fluctuate with criticism and pushback during a negotiation. Pushback is expected for everyone and is also a technique used by the other side. You may encounter criticism, but don't take it personally and don't say anything you might regret later. Moderate your emotions and try to keep the mood positive and calm. Just continue to make the points you prepared. Making the point will show the other person they failed in ruining your composure.

Tip:

An essential practice that will help you with being confident is doing your research and being prepared.

Length of the Negotiation

Some say that men are impatient and want to get to the point and that women will take more time to "make it right." Although I highly doubt that's the only intention. Everyone wants things to go right; in a reasonable amount of time. Nobody wants a negotiation to go on forever. You have to assess each person individually to gauge what they are comfortable with. If you rush a negotiation, chances are you won't get the right end of the deal. Take the time you need that will increase your chances of success. The Socratic method can be useful. Sometimes inching people forward is more effective.

Tip:

Most negotiations take several sessions or steps. Some negotiations are actually ongoing, for quite long periods of time, months or even years for really big deals. You probably won't get any major negotiations done in one meeting.

Relationships

Again, some say that women worry more about protecting relationships with the people they're negotiating, while men see negotiating as an opportunity to show off their skills and ultimately win. Women have to "think" (not worry) about this because it could be a real hurdle. Meaning, you need to consider the ego of everyone at the table. Your goal should be to walk away with most of what you want. Opinions of what people think about you are important but secondary. Respect and likeability are great, but I wouldn't sacrifice the negotiation for it. The reality is you can be/act as respectful and likable as you can, but that does not preclude others will perceive you as such. You can't please everyone, especially in a tough negotiation. Here's the thing, not everyone will like you, regardless of gender. Depending on the degree to which you will interact during and after the negotiation should dictate your concern. Meaning, if you are negotiating with respect, and people don't like you afterward, and this means something to you, do you want to be doing business with them? Are these the people you want to be in bed with?

Tip: Depending on if the negotiation is a one-time deal or an ongoing relationship determines the level to which you prioritize the relationship

Those are just the baseline, there is much more to good negotiation tactics, persuasion strategies and reading people. Those books exist in abundance and I encourage anyone to read as much as you can to learn and improve.

Chris Voss in his book, *NEVER SPLIT THE DIFFERENCE: NEGOTIATING AS IF YOUR LIFE DEPENDED ON IT*, presents strategies that are practical, universal, and not gender-specific at all. He refers to the tone of voice, body language, helping people feel safe and protected, using empathy. Understanding the emotions of people over precise terms seems ultimately more important. It does boil down to people's emotions at the end of the day, and building rapport and trust are essential.

A point of view that we keep encountering is that men are unethical, and women are more ethical. But what exactly are the characteristics of unethical behavior? And what demographic are these men? Various men surround me, and a good number are supreme examples of ethical beings. Study after study shows that women are more ethical than men, in most cases. However, I question the cases of study, mostly because we do not have many women in high level, high ranking, decision making positions, over a long enough period of time to see if they would be more ethical on the whole? Could it be the case that the world was different before and that more men will be more ethical in the future? This reason why this is important when it comes to negotiation and Sexual Intelligence in Business is because the lens to which you look through, determines how you perceive. If you go into negotiations with the viewpoint that all men are unethical and ready to harass you, and that all women are ethical and will never screw you in a negotiation, you will not be fully prepared and you may not come out of that negotiation with what you want.

When one looks back at historical revolutions, resistance movements, and collective action, they all started with great intentions. Still, by the time they overthrow and gain power, they often repeat the exact unethical actions and behaviors. Until more women hold high power positions, determining whether one gender is more ethical than the other should remain inconclusive.

In academia and business, negotiations are viewed as isolated events where victory goes to the party that scores the best deal, financial or otherwise. But negotiations don't happen in a vacuum. Often, the parties involved—a customer, a vendor, or an employee—are engaged in an established relationship. Research has shown, for example, that women's economic outcomes do not differ from those of men when negotiating on behalf of others. Still, the perception that they are incapable of advocating effectively for themselves remains influential.

When considering academic studies on negotiations, we have to keep in mind the studies are simulated, often with students as study participants, which is not entirely reflective of real-world situations, behind closed doors. Simulations serve as good practice, but as unrealistic measuring tools for gender differences for several reasons, including the fact that the stakes for participants are low relative to the career-ending risks working professionals can face at the negotiating table. Higher stakes are likely to homogenize behavior. Because simulations are also typically set up as game-like competitions, the value of collaboration and problem solving required of real-world negotiations gets overlooked. In the real world, generating goodwill through problem-solving, is necessary for striking agreements. In fabricated settings, participants treat the negotiation as a one-shot interaction, which means relationships among participants are seen as short term and, therefore, expendable. Not to mention, that underlying women's perception as poor negotiators is a fundamental flaw in how negotiating success is studied and measured.

Perceived gender differences in negotiation performance are commonly invoked as one explanation for the disparities. In perpetuation, the false proposition that women are incompetent negotiators becomes a reality simply because people believe it. In turn, this reality perpetuates a vicious cycle of "reign of terror" in which women's poor performance in one negotiation is proof of future incompetence.

Growth mindsets allow us to move past the biology vs. culture debate.

The most current research suggested that differences in outcomes are situational. In a 2015 meta-analysis, Mazzei et al. found that women perform as well as men under three conditions: when negotiating on behalf of another person (but not a larger entity), when given information about the bargaining range and had experience with negotiation. Under these circumstances, men not only lost any advantage but also underperformed women. Overall, the gender difference in economic outcomes was so variable that the authors concluded, "A single overall true gender difference does not exist."

It's not about blaming women for injustices; it's all about a performance mindset. Positive thinking. They are reprogramming limiting beliefs.

There is another type of barrier preventing women from being recognized as skilled negotiators on par with men. In general, society values negotiation prowess in ways favoring decidedly masculine traits, such as assertiveness, a focus on self-interest, and the ability to think and act rationally. So, when scholars and others set out to evaluate who is successful at negotiating and who is not, they conceptualize and measure performance based on what they consider to be correct and objective characteristics of effective negotiations. But is this viewpoint accurate? No.

According to Mirvis, "there is a growing consensus that organizations with cultures grounded in integrity make ethical behavior everybody's responsibility, and this builds stronger relationships between a company, its employees, and other stakeholders." Recognize that negotiation skills are learned. Gender stereotypes hold that women negotiators are innately ineffective, but extensive research dispels these assumptions. Men and women become effective negotiators through hard work and practice, not genetics.

One thing that was consistent amongst the research was calls for changing the narrative on what it means to be a successful negotiator. Our success metrics are severely outdated. Currently, men and women exhibit slightly different negotiating styles, still acting out their socially constructed identities, but with a substantial agreement in style. Patriarchal assumptions about masculine superiority obscure some of how *stereotypical* feminine strengths are essential to effective negotiating. Gender differences fluctuate systematically, and savvy negotiators utilize both masculine and feminine approaches to get to yes. My only wish is that we call them just approaches, not masculine or feminine, but approaches.

While possible, changing the negotiation paradigm is not easy. Gender stereotypes, and the misguided assumption that they are warranted, are hard to overcome. Doing so requires academics to conduct their research into gender differences differently. Women and men negotiators to think about their roles in new ways, and innovative leaders to instil a new mindset in their organizations and people in general to drop this gender assigned characteristics. According to Schoemaker and Tetlock, highly creative people are willing to push new ways of thinking. "Breakthrough innovations," they write, "often come from mavericks willing to reject convention and hierarchy."

Don't wait for someone to offer you a raise. You must speak up and ask for what you want in life. It's up to you to ensure you get what you want and deserve.

Lastly, I think by now we can see the striking parallels of how men and women are negotiating in the boardroom as well as the bedroom. Mutual sexual satisfaction is something that needs to be negotiated in the bedroom and research shows women are reluctant to do that as well. If you have blazing sexual differences, then an open discussion is critical to the negotiation process. A willingness to explore the issues surrounding sexual interests and desires, you need to clearly articulate what you want and expect. Sex remains a tricky topic to bring up at the best of times. When women feel a disparage between their desires and what is expected of them, they often react with just declining sex, have unwanted sex (feeling the pressure), faking orgasm, or feeling disappointed and remaining silent. This reflects how women imagine their right to ask for, or decline, sex. Implications for power, coercion, and sexual entitlement are at play here. This is reflective and a microcosm for women in business. We can draw parallels between how women negotiate in business and the bedroom. Women are more sexually satisfied when they ask for what they want. The bedroom is a place to claim your rights, demand your pleasure and orgasm for real! You can actually use the negotiation strategies in a similar way. This will also give you the confidence to negotiate in business AND it actually helps men to learn about equity in the bedroom.

Let's not forget, men are just as self-conscious in the bedroom, deep down. According to Dr. Sarah Hunter Murray in her article Heterosexual Men's Sexual Desire: Supported by, or Deviating from, Traditional Masculinity Norms and Sexual Scripts?, she suggests that "researchers, therapists, and sex educators be mindful that men face pressures to exhibit sexual desire in stereotypically masculine ways and that outward demonstrations of sexual interest may not always be accurate representations of men's true experiences". Men do their fair share of acting out gender roles, even when they don't want to.

CHAPTER 7

IDENTITY IRRECONCILABLE DIFFERENCES

The Challenges on Identity

It all starts with the existential question, who am I? What is my purpose in life? But then it quickly devolves into our natural inclination to categorize. Suddenly, we're in a box. There is so much one can be, so specific you can get with your identity in modern times, which can come with various benefits. The downside, though, is that the process lends itself too easily to othering and "out-grouping", and by different orders of magnitude. Identity often breeds conflict and may be more problematic than its worth.

WHAT IS IDENTITY

So, what does it mean to have an identity? This is a somewhat enigmatic subject. Identity is a set of characteristics, interests, or attributes from which one may derive a sense of self and of belonging, self-respect, an affinity towards others, a label or categorization, often related to cultural norms and society. The concept is complex, and coming up with exact definitions is hotly debated within academia. Another area of debate surrounds to what extent identity is socially constructed or not. To what degree is it learned behavior compared to a degree of agency one has in adopting chosen identities for themselves?. It's probably a blend of all these things, which could be perhaps why it's so hard to define precisely.

How does this relate to Sexual Intelligence in Business The immediate connection is the most obvious: the

#metoo movement. We are looking at gender equity pertaining to power relations in terms of promotions, equal pay, mentorship, opportunities, and abuse of power in sexual harassment and sexual violence. Gender and sexual preference being the most visible and relevant identities in this context. But many different identities are playing out in business and the workplace, beyond feminine and masculine. When we use gender, often people think of that in terms of a man and a woman. Just for reference, the definitions in this context are that sex refers to biological attributes (usually male/female but also a range based on genes, chromosomes). Gender are socially constructed roles, behaviors, expressions and identities, with a wide range of categories.

Since the beginning of humanity, it has been the case that not everyone neatly fits into one or the other, but a more recent notion is that we are asking the question, why should we fit into those?

There are even more connections to the intersection such as sexual proclivities (degree of libido), sexual interests, relationship compositions, monogamous or polygamous, which can get tied up into religious identities. We also have a work or business identity, such as manager, boss, employee, client. These strongly define how we interact and treat each other. Are you quiet or outgoing, ambitious or satisfied? Are you a flirt or awkward, social, paranoid, fearful? We can probably list hundreds of other identity-related traits and corresponding characteristics that we match with identities, because whether we are at work or doing business, we are also who we are; at the moment anyways. I do not believe that we effectively separate personal from professional. Further to that, we are animals with biological imperatives. To think that we can erase all this from business and the workplace is, well, next to impossible. When it comes to being respectful and empathic, and reading people, this is often done by assessing identity. Being aware of ourselves, and what position we come from, vis-a-vis others, affects how we think of others and how we treat them. If identity is that on which we base our assessments, this can lead too much towards assumptions and this is where things can go very wrong.

This makes me wonder if we should challenge the concept of identity altogether.

How badly do we need it?

In his book titled Preparing for Peace, Conflict Transformation Class, John Paul Lederach writes that all conflicts are identity conflicts. And yet, according to the renowned psychologist Abraham Maslow, he marks identity as one of the most important of basic human needs. What a quagmire!

Let's also examine why gender roles and gender characteristics are an antiquated categorization system and how the concept of "identity" may be detrimental. We should also consider why stomping down on men is not an ideal pathway to uplifting and empowering women.

THE PROBLEMS CAUSED BY IDENTITY

When referring to men's identity, most notably white men, one must be careful. We cannot overlook the irony here. Those who built the western society we know now, despite its many shortcomings, is a far better lifestyle than ancient times, albeit recognizing the treachery of colonization. For most of western history, the white man has had it pretty good, indeed. But going to war and pre-industrial labour work wasn't all sunshine and lollipops either. Chasing animals with spears, chopping down trees, building houses, and farming land so that everyone could eat and sleep is what most men were doing. Today, we know those same men are good guys: Nice, funny, loving, ethical, good parents, productive members of society. However, there's that percentage of "white male" (and all other kinds of males) that hasn't been so nice. To be blunt, they have been everything along the spectrum from disrespectful to entirely brutal, not just to women, but to many other human beings of all kinds. That is well-documented in history, and that still counts for today.

At the same time, women are not perfect, either. We are all human and capable of being nasty, unethical, and all sorts of negative characteristics and behaviors. Feminist movements sometimes give the impression that all women are great and deserve all the opportunities simply because they are women and not because they are capable, qualified, and intelligent human beings, which they are and we don't need to prove that anymore. What this also entails is not shaming either.

We have entered a confusing time. Chivalry, historically instituted as a code of conduct for religious piety or military or as social norms that have adapted over time, still partially exist today. Embodied in chivalry was a sense of moral obligation to protect, and that somehow made an odd leap to modern society as "gentlemen" who define a code of conduct towards women, who, of course, were believed to be unable to protect themselves. But in the 20th century, it translates into opening doors and paying for dinner. Let's take the "who pays for dinner" example, in a romantic and heteronormative context. Since different people hold different value systems and perceive situations differently, this can lead to confusion in gender relations. Men used to order for the women at a restaurant, now the woman gets to choose. Can women order for men? Maybe that feels emasculating for some, a nice change of pace for others. Most women still want the man to pay for dinner, but not always. There's more dutch these days, but it still needs to be sorted out each time. Plus, it's not always the man/woman binary composition. Some women I know love it when they feel "protected" by men; other women feel wholly insulted. I'm not suggesting to come up with a rubric that everyone can follow from now on, even if we could. Using an everyday example, I'm trying to illustrate how something as simple as paying for dinner is now complicated. We need to be gracious and empathetic with each other. We need to teach, learn, and grow with patience and kindness as we transition into a new phase of humanity.

The role of women in the world is changing. Girls today are positively encouraged and told that they could do anything, be anyone, not just someone's wife. They are absorbing this message, which is excellent. Women today are the beneficiaries of decades of affirmations and achievements made by past and ongoing feminist movements. Women's voices are heard (for the most part); negative experiences are beginning to be believed (more now than before, although there's work to be done here). But are we encouraging our boys in a way that is good for them too? Are we making as much effort in teaching our boys to be respectful, empathetic individuals? William Liu, Ph.D., a professor of counselling psychology at the University of Iowa, who studies masculinity, writes that masculine "ideals" might feel threatened, consciously or otherwise, by societal shifts, including the increasingly powerful role of women in the workplace or the growing acceptance of same-sex relationships. "The culture is changing, and it no longer privileges [the stereotypical male] point of view," says Liu.

I'd like to discourage anyone who feels a "male movement" is in order, but it would seem logical that boys also need to learn how to navigate toward a full expression of their potential, respectfully and equitably. Yes, the patriarchal system advances men automatically, but that is changing. If we are trying to rewire the system away from patriarchy and towards a new system, we don't want to flip things so far that we then have the same problem for men in the future, as we had for women. We should be treating all children equally, as human beings, in as much of an unbiased, non-gender specific kind of way. That is what will help everyone.

Y. Joel Wong, Ph.D., a professor of counselling psychology at Indiana University Bloomington, found that overall, men who conformed to traditional masculine norms had higher rates of mental health problems such as depression, anxiety and stress, and lower rates of positive mental health outcomes, such as life satisfaction, self-esteem and psychological well-being. In particular, Wong found conformity to three masculine norms—playboy behavior, power over women and self-reliance—were significantly linked to psychological maladjustment. That suggests that sexist attitudes might have detrimental effects on men's mental health, Wong says. Many adult and young men feel trapped in an outdated masculinity model, measured by strength and physical prowess, and not allowed to be vulnerable without being deemed weak. Manliness is about having power over others; they don't necessarily have the language or the forum to talk about how they feel, not even amongst their male friends. They are asking themselves, what does it mean to be a man? And is that important anymore? Is this worth risking mental health?

Many men feel isolated, confused, and conflicted about their natures, to the extent that "nature" dictates. Many think that the very qualities used to define them — their strength, aggression, and competitiveness — are no longer wanted, needed, if they identified with those at all. Many others never felt strong or aggressive or competitive in the first place. It's a false assumption that all men think that. Men don't have a masculinity model that allows for fear or grief or tenderness or sadness that sometimes overtakes us all.

"What it means to be a man today is different than what it meant 20 years ago," says James O'Neil, Ph.D., a psychologist at the University of Connecticut who studies gender role conflict. "There's a paradigm shift occurring in our country regarding what it means to be masculine, and many men have had difficulty adjusting to that transition."

Men are reporting a hard time trying to find that balance in their relationships, and the behaviors are not having the desired results of their partner's satisfaction, happiness, and appreciation. I've had many conversations with men about this. They feel it is a "no-win situation" in dating, business, and the workplace. It affects everyone. When men try to be "good guys," they sometimes feel mistreated and disrespected. If they follow more assertive strategies, they are labeled "jerks" and "players"—who may get laid but do not receive the love or respect they desire. If it was not evident, one thing to point out is the perception of being "taken advantage of, mistreated, and disrespected." Regardless of the degree or the frequency of which this happens, men do experience this as well. Some women mistreat men. Oh yes, I said it. Do "all women" do this? Of course not, but this is the danger of discrimination, stereotypes, and making statements that apply to a broad group of people. It also relates to the risk of forming such a strong and distinct identity. We get boxed in; we get grouped, we get typecast. We get compared, and we compare ourselves. We get "othered, and we do some othering ourselves. These stereotypes and situations occur in business, but in ways not talked about much.

A recent Harvard Business Review study in 2017, found that conservative men become more conservative when their status is threatened. They double-down on tradition vs. working to compensate. This is interesting because I can completely attest to this in my personal life. At first, my husband was resistant. Despite all my warnings of not being a traditional woman, we slid into roles once the kids were born, and he was quite comfortable with that. The more my business ramped up, the more my husband had to take on some of the "traditionally woman tasks", not without some "encouragement" and coaching, but we got there. It didn't happen like magic. It happened because I fought for it. I advocated for myself. He learned, empathized, and low and behold, we made it work. I didn't wait for society to do it for me. Did we fight and argue about it? Yes. Are all these things easy? Nope. Are they doable? Totally. We have to be willing to stand up for what we want, each and every time.

In his book, *Who Stole My Spear (2017)*, Tim Samuels explains how the modern man struggles with his identity. He states that yes, men have it easier, they are still masters of the universe, and they populate 95 percent of FTSE CEO positions and over 70 percent of parliaments. Men are often blissfully unaware of glass ceilings for women and are trying in all sorts of ways to channel their apparent insatiable sex drives. Notwithstanding, we may have a silent modern crisis on our hands, that we've yet to imagine how that may play out in the future.

Now, I realize that for many women who have had some extremely horrible experiences that they may have a hard time empathizing. Some even believe that men should feel the burn, suffer a bit, so they "get it". We are all grappling with new roles and identities. A Pew Research study, conducted Sept. 15-Oct. 13, 2015, showed that "among 1,807 U.S. parents with children younger than 18, [...] in two-parent families, parenting and household responsibilities are shared more equally when both the mother and the father work full time than when the father is employed full time and the mother is employed part time or not employed. But even in households where both parents work full time, many say a large share of the day-to-day parenting responsibilities falls to mothers."

We often forget that there is as much competition, labeling, judging, and discrimination amongst women and men themselves. Men have been battling each other for millennia. It's a cold war between women. On the outside, women play nice. Let's help each other, ban together, women's empowerment. But this is not always the case. Sometimes it is. Sometimes it's not. The point is, there are battles and differences between the genders, as well as within. Knowing this, how much can we say that identity matters here? Is this just a human thing?

Changing social norms has placed an interesting conundrum on everyone, both acceptable as relationship partners and attractive as sex partners. Consequently, many needs are unfulfilled, and a big part of this is an effort to mitigate that. The implications are more than just sexual gratification, although that is pretty darn important. People tend to use the colloquial saying that men are from Mars and women are from Venus, to account for the many differences between the sexes. But I think we should be focusing our efforts on how we can live, interact, love, have sex, and do business together, here on Earth. It will just take effort and mutual understanding. The Sexual Intelligence in Business framework can help with that.

Can we imagine a world where we can adjust to situations accordingly? Where we can be who we want to be at that time. Humans are multidimensional beings, and I think we underestimate our capacity to be fluid. We are referring back to the concept of grey thinking. We all encompass both complementary and contradictory characteristics. Perhaps consider how you act and speak to your children, friends, parents, business associates, and lovers. We say different things to them; we use other words and tone, and discuss different topics. Doesn't that tell us something?

Men on the one hand are feeling that they are restricted in saying what they think, what they want, or asking for what they need, and on the other being encouraged to open up and share their feelings. At the same time, depending on what circles you run in, men are also being encouraged and supported to actually identify and share their feelings and to "be themselves". Women have been trying to get men to express their emotions for years! We all should be able to speak out, develop the language and skills to do so, and have the safe spaces in which this can be done. The mental health issues that men are experiencing are not trivial. They need to have the same level of consideration about what they are up against

- frustration and isolating feelings, crime, and mental wellness issues.

A report by the mental health charity CALM (the Campaign Against Living Miserably), seeks to address why male suicide rates are high. The CALM report, A Crisis in Modern Masculinity: Understanding the Causes of Male Suicide, present and analysis of the pressures and expectations that men and women face in their daily lives. They concluded that men are failing to cope and keeping their problems hidden from others. CALM's chief executive Jane Powell said: "The research underlines that so often men are their own worst enemies, men need new rules for survival. Outmoded, incorrect, and misplaced male self-beliefs prove lethal, and the traditional strong, silent response to adversity is increasingly failing to protect men from themselves."

HOW CAN WE OVERCOME THIS?

Men could benefit from relieving themselves from the burden of believing their value in a relationship is financial rather than emotional. Even better, why don't we all support and encourage each other in all areas? Finance is not the domain of men, and emotions are not the domain of women. They belong to everyone.

We can't always blame culture here. We want to avoid ethnocentric thinking patterns that assume that since this is a problem for "us" (presuming this means western culture), then it is also a problem for others. Even more succinctly, there also isn't a grand description that counts for all westerners. What is western culture really? Recognizing differences, intersections, history, culture, and systems is crucial for the effectiveness of efforts to resolve issues. When it comes to assigning characteristics to men and women, this is quite problematic. I consider it to not be useful, and is the foundation of many of the issues that we face today. Ascribing to gender, sex, religion, culture may be an avenue towards entrenching racism, sexism, all the bad "isms." Language matters, and it's one thing to display behaviors, but the speed at which the mind associates terms unconsciously dictates our behavior.

Here's the kicker: when a man or a woman is ascribed with a characteristic they like, prefer, or makes them feel good, nobody argues or contests it. For example: women are smarter; women are better at multitasking; women make better negotiators. Will that be argued? The problem is, you can't have it both ways. Either you reject broad sweeping generalizations, or you don't.

Gender norms reinforce perceptions of women being nurturing, weak, and emotional. Now, these attributes are not inherently harmful, but there are implications here. The idea that women are more nurturing assigns them as nature's choice to raise the kids and choose between motherhood or a career. Plus, they need to cater to their "less capable" husbands with unpaid household labour; it becomes clear that gender norms are not harmless, imagined things. On the contrary, they cause genuine problems for everyone.

Men suffer the consequences of gender norms in a similar way. They reinforce the idea that men are aggressive, tough, and primitive. The impacts are that men are often unable to express their emotions in healthy ways, and their mental health and interpersonal relationships are impaired due to this. Gender norms are, in many ways, a losing game, and modern feminism has not let this go unnoticed. Some Feminist and varied academic work attempts to dispel the myth that women and men have naturally and generalizable differences, aptitudes, and abilities. We need to acknowledge the depth and breadth of emotions experienced by men and women, encouraging them to accept and express them. But we also need to recognize that there are differences. Beyond the obvious physical differences, are there other differences that we have not yet been able to determine if its biology or social construction, the whole nature vs. nurture debate?

Matters of anatomy notwithstanding — there isn't anything a man can do that a woman cannot. Whether women want to do those things (that a man can do) is a different matter altogether. And the vice versa. Much of what we assign to gender roles is a matter of skill, instruction, and cognitive ability, endowed upon humans inasmuch plenty and randomness that nature can muster. It's a conditioning, which can (and should be) undone. We are all capable creatures. Why do we perpetuate the notion that a man's value in relationships is his ability to provide and protect women who are perfectly capable of this? Why has the concept of a man's worth, willingness to act as an engaged, equal partner, promote and support personal growth, and develop those they love, not translated completely? When we think about it, we cannot ask men or women to change overnight. There is a process to untrain and re-train ourselves. We all have many things to "undo," but the process can start immediately. Feminism and the respective movements have expanded our idea of what a woman can do and be. At the same time, we are redefining what it means to be a man. Or, perhaps, we need to redefine what makes a good human.

While some people are waiting for a new equilibrium, others can just go right ahead and start acting as they think is right, educate ourselves, modifying our behaviors, inspiring others. We do not need to wait for social norms or evolved standards of attractiveness to get sexual fulfillment. One thing that I've noticed during my research and conversations is that many people are sitting back and waiting for society to change. This is a backward strategy because society is a collection of actors. You must take responsibility for your actions. Mahatma Gandhi said, "You must be the change you wish to see in the world." Waiting for change until you start behaving the way you should be, is counter-productive.

According to incentive theories on motivation, we seek out rewards and avoid punishments. When rewards outweigh penalties, people perform behaviors. When punishment weighs more heavily, people avoid those same behaviors. Invest in yourself, value, and success. Treat partners, co-workers, business relationships, equitably, and respectfully. Don't sell yourself short for less than you deserve. This approach takes constant effort, through owning your standards, keeping motivated, and inspiring others to do the same. It also requires patience (in time and towards people) and loads of intellectual effort.

We are in a social flux period, with an abundance of opportunities to satisfy ourselves professionally, socially, and biologically. If you feel like you're struggling between conflicting demands and motivations, find your unique way to adapt. Better yet, carve a pathway that others can adopt; there's a leadership opportunity here. Dating and relationships, personally, professionally, in business, can be tricky and can involve costs and trade-offs. Double-binds can be explained, but don't need to be adopted. You have choices here.

Everyone needs to get comfortable with themselves, flaws and all, the good, the bad and the ugly. It's time to let go of these destructive identities. The key is to let go that which does not serve you. The Buddhism saying invites you to drop it like a hot piece of coal.

I conclude this chapter with a few related quotes to reflect on before moving to the next chapter:

"All conflicts are identity conflicts..." -- John Paul Lederach.

"As we uncover our true nature, we realize all those things we have attached to our identity are merely labels to realize that a sense of place in the world. Moreover, I create a false sense of self to form an image of who they think I am. Discarding the false self is a call to abandon the beliefs and thoughts of who you think you are in discovering a stronger sense of self". - Tony Fahrky, Mission.org

"True self is non-self, the awareness that the self is made only of non-self elements. There's no separation between self and other, and everything is interconnected. Once you are aware of that, you are no longer caught in the idea that you are a separate entity." — Thich Nhat Hanh.

"You wouldn't worry so much about what others think of you if you realized how seldom they do," said Eleanor Roosevelt, American politician and activist.

CHAPTER 8

ALTERED STATES AND THE SCIENCE BEHIND PRODUCTIVITY

Sexual desire is among the most powerful of human desires. With this intense drive energizing us, everyone can ride that wave and use your body's neurochemical reactions to manifest incredible qualities and states of mind. These include enhanced visualization, clarity, creativity, imagination, courage, motivation, and willpower, and ability to persist despite all obstacles and difficulties. Our sexual energy is so formidable that some say it is the source behind almost all creative achievements considered "genius." Sex has the potential to increase your inventiveness capability and creative verve to the point where you are unstoppable. Plus, so much more! How you ask? Let's explore...

We go to great extents to make ourselves appear intelligent and attractive. When we take away the facade, these extents can actually be driven by an underlying quest for love, sexual pleasure and signaling to a desirable mate. This does not mean that we are compromising ourselves, it just means that we understand the importance of it. If a tree falls in a forest, would anybody care if it was pretty? Society and increasingly antiquated power systems have programmed us to think of sex in terms of reproduction and propagation of family genetics, nothing more than a means to an end. But deep inside, many of us long for love and sex like nothing else in the world. I'm not discounting those who may feel asexual or struggle with libido, I mean deep, deep down. We could even go as far as to say that our thirst for power or ambition for success is the true means to an end because we hope these will bring us love and sexual pleasure. Let's look at why sex is so important and how it can be used to improve your business and career.

According to a study published in The Journal of Sex Research, men, on average, think about sex nineteen times per day, whereas women, on average, think about sex ten times per day. Regardless of where you fall on this spectrum, thinking about sex ten to nineteen times per day is significant. Don't get hung up on the exact numbers, because honestly, it's so damn hard to study subjective behaviors. They could be lying to the researcher, they could be lying to themselves, or the thoughts are in passing and hard to count. And those are averages, which means some think about it much less and others much more! Sex and its accompanying imagery are inescapable; beyond the fact that its on our minds, it's in advertising, television, movies, magazines, and the internet. Empires throughout history rise and fall for love and sex, and people go into massive consumer debt (cars, plastic surgery, expensive clothes, cosmetics, porn hub subscriptions, etc.), people risk their jobs, professions, and families for a roll in the hay. When we look to pop-culture, this theme remains pretty consistent -- back in 2012, a study that said 92 percent of the 174 songs that made it onto Billboard's Top 10 had sexual or reproductive references.

Besides reproduction, sex is essential and is ultimately about intimacy, pleasure, and/or sexual expression. Sex (in its many forms) has many positive intellectual, physical, emotional, and social benefits. Physically, an active sex life provides benefits, including a youthful appearance and a healthy lifestyle. Not only does sex burn calories (100 calories burned every 30 minutes), but people who have sex regularly have higher levels of the antibody called immunoglobulin A (IgA). According to a study by Dr. Carl Charnetski of the Department of Psychology at Wilkes University in Wilkes-Barre, Pennsylvania, IgA combats disease and keeps the body safe from colds and flu. Sex can help you sleep better, which creates a more robust immune system. Oxytocin released during orgasm promotes restful sleep, decreases heart problems in both women and men, and helps with pain control. For women, increased sexual activity leads to experiencing lighter periods with fewer cramps and makes their period finish faster. It lowers blood pressure, improves bladder control, and is connected to a reduction in prostate cancer for men and protection from endometriosis for women. Sex rejuvenates, makes us less prone to illnesses, reduces the risk of stroke, and fights the aging process too! And ladies, having orgasms will give you the perfect anti-aging method no lab could ever produce, bottle, or sell! HELLO! A hormone called DHEA is produced during sex, helping with various things, including your skin. So, throw down those anti-aging products and hop into bed! Just kidding, don't stop the products. They probably help too.

Having a satisfying sex life is intimately correlated with overall quality of life. The increase in sex raises your sense of well-being and self-fulfillment. Dr. Laura Berman, Ph.D., Obstetrician-Gynecologist, and Psychiatrist at the Feinberg School of Medicine at Northwestern University, and Dr. Jennifer Berman, MD., Urology and Director of the Female Sexual Medicine Center at the UCLA Medical Center co-authored a book where they discuss how orgasms can reduce stress. In "For Women Only: A Revolutionary Guide to Reclaiming Your Sex Life". They provide women with crucial information about their bodies and sexual responses. They say that orgasms can reduce stress by releasing endorphins that activate pleasure centers in the brain, which create feelings of intimacy and a relaxed state of mind that ultimately wards off depression. When sex life is great, confidence will increase in other areas of life. According to sex therapist Sandor Gardos, "When things go well in bed, you feel more confident and powerful in other parts of your life, making us more daring and uninhibited in life. It boosts our self-esteem, our sense of feeling attractive, desirable, proficient, and confident."

While we can lust for someone we are attracted to, the attraction itself is more distinct. It involves the brain pathways that control "reward" behavior, which partly explains why the beginning of a relationship can be exhilarating and even all-consuming. The attraction seems to lead to lower serotonin, a hormone known to be involved in appetite and mood. That's why having a crush on someone is so awesome, the best diet ever. Serotonin is one of love's most important chemicals and one that may render us temporarily insane.

Interestingly, low serotonin levels are what underlies the overpowering infatuation that characterizes the beginning stages of love. The original survival instinct, of having as many offspring as possible, is no longer in strong effect: Maslow's pyramid say what? Still, when we receive the affection of a desirable person, sex increases blood flow, and since intimate sex involves a lot of kissing, kissing encourages saliva. Why in the hell would we want more saliva, you ask? Because saliva cleans food debris between the teeth and lowers the level of acidity in your mouth. Admittedly, this sounds a bit unsexy, but why not embrace all the peripheral benefits of sex?

The absolute, hands down reason, in my humble opinion, is because sex releases kick-ass neurochemicals and increases blood flow to the brain, which means that you'll be more alert. If you have a lot of work to accomplish or projects to complete, having sex beforehand could help you. There is some evidence that shows people who often think about sex had better critical thinking skills. As athletes use visualization to win, can sexual fantasies serve a similar function? There are loads of data out there to show that sex is good for us, but it's also good for business. *Bachai, Sabrina. "The Top 10 Reasons Why Sex Is Good For You." Medical Daily. N.p., 20 May 2013. Web. 28 Jan. 2015,* shows that the neurochemicals produce by sex and like activities, it makes us more productive and maybe even smarter! Some researchers also postulate that sexual activity is associated with better cognitive abilities in older adults (Padoani et al., 2000; Wright and Jenna, 2016; Wright et al., 2017). This could mean there is a correlation between sexual activity and healthy brain cell growth.

Researchers from anthropology to neuroscience have been trying to nail down the science behind love and attraction. As you would expect, most of what they say reads as 'obvious' and at the same time complex, abstract, and sometimes uncomfortably predestined. As you may predict, there are two sides to the story, or probably even more. Researchers tend to err on the side of caution, avoiding drawing firm conclusions. It can be challenging to make decisions and take positions based on nuance; I get that. Sometimes people follow blindly, because it takes a lot of effort to unpack and repack information, and it's often just more efficient to grab what someone else says and go with that. But everyone would be well served to evaluate the information for themselves. Going through the exercise and intellectual effort is important. Ultimately, sex, love, and attraction are complicated, dynamic, and very subjective, but there's a lot of gold in there.

The neurochemicals are the activators of your sexual energy and eros life force.

Here's what we do know. Love can be explained by chemistry, and there's a bit of a formula involved. It's of course related to finding someone attractive, not just that you identify/label that person as good looking or sexy, but that you feel attracted to them from a biological standpoint. Like a magnetic pull, a punch in the gut, slap in the face, your body reacts, even before you've barely exchanged words. Many of us have looked at someone and said to ourselves how beautiful or gorgeous they are, physically as a human specimen. But that is different from when you feel something, a little (or big) sensation in your stomach (yeah, butterflies!) your heart races, blood pumps, and temperature rises. It can get as intense as feeling nauseous, speech impaired, sweating, chest pounds, can't walk, can't think, and it kind of feels like your brain doesn't work, but it's just the opposite. That is where the saying *love is blind* comes in. If taken individually, all those 'conditions' of attraction sound terrible, but it's one of the GREATEST feelings in the world. It is within that state, those feelings, that sexual energy, that you could use and channel.

For centuries, people thought love and emotions came from the heart. In reality, love is all about the brain – which produces chemicals that can make your body go wild! Which is delightful! According to a team of scientists led by Dr. Helen Fisher at Rutgers, romantic love can be broken down into lust, attraction, and attachment. Of course, there are intersections and nuances. Each type is characterized by its own set of hormones; testosterone and estrogen drive lust; dopamine, norepinephrine, and serotonin create attraction; and oxytocin and vasopressin mediate attachment.

To summarize, let's start with lust. The desire for sexual gratification drives lust. The evolutionary basis for this stems from our biological imperative to reproduce, subject to all living things. Organisms must pass on their genes, and thus contribute to the perpetuation of their species. Why is this motivation so strong? Keeping our DNA alive is more complicated than you'd expect. Survival rates are low, and our genes are easily eradicated from the face of the Earth. The hypothalamus section in the brain produces sex hormones testosterone and estrogen from the testes and ovaries, which drives sexual desire. While these chemicals are often gender-stereotyped, both genders are affected, and testosterone increases libido in just about everyone. The hypothalamus relates to the regulation of emotions and the production of dopamine, oxytocin, and vasopressin. Lust is very primal, which makes sense in the context of the "spreading the seed" biological motivation. This affects both genders but it should not come as a surprise that its more pronounced in men, which can account for explanations by men who claim to enjoy sex with someone and not care about them. Although, I would argue women have the same capacity but appear to be less prone to exercise that capacity, not to mention that researchers have possibly been less inclined to study them!

It was different when men and women were partially separated (home vs. work), then you add mixed genders in the office, a contained environment, like boxing up two wild animals expecting them not to "fuck or fight".

Dopamine is of particular importance in the brain's reward pathway. It is released when we do things that feel good to us, such as, but not limited to, spending time with loved ones and guess what? Having sex. The brain releases high levels of norepinephrine (aka adrenaline) and dopamine during attraction. These pleasant neurochemicals make us kooky, slaphappy, exhilarated, and euphoric, even leading to a loss of appetite and insomnia – again, the idea that you are so "in love" you can't eat and can't sleep. Norepinephrine, which is related to the "fight or flight" response, kicks into high gear when we're stressed and keeps us alert. In the attraction stage, dopamine is stimulated by the "chase" aspect of love. It's also triggered when a baby hears its mother's footsteps, or when your phone vibes with a notification! Dopamine alerts us that our needs are about to be met.

Again, low serotonin levels are what underlies the overpowering infatuation that characterizes the beginning stages of love. The original survival instinct, of having as many offspring as possible, is no longer in strong effect. Still, when we receive the affection of a desirable individual, loads of serotonin is generated. And when we are on the receiving end of admiration, that pumps serotonin too. It feels so good that people tend to seek it repeatedly. Desirability is part of what drives flirting in business/workplace, and this is how flirting can lead to co-workers or professionals engaging in sexual relationships or affairs and infidelity. The power lies in controlling and channeling that. You can ride that energy and feed off it to accelerate your business, projects, and feeling super high about life. Additionally, one need not move past this stage. You can simply swim around in these feelings and feed off the energy without ever pursuing a relationship in reality.

Interestingly and relevant here is that lust and attraction partly shut off the brain's prefrontal cortex, including rational behavior! This sounds bad but it's actually good. Because it's this "rational" thinking that sometimes prevents us from taking risks. If we always listened to this, we wouldn't jump off diving boards, skydive, or take on a new job / quit a job to start a new business. This state of mind that lust and attraction invoke is where we can access altered states of consciousness. But it does require a mature, skilled, and intentional response. We have all had our fair share of irrational behavior when it comes to these love chemicals. However, with awareness and intent, we can take all the best sides and avoid the pitfalls.

It's like eating a great meal: don't overeat, or you'll feel like shit.

It is understandable that there can be an inclination to let it all go and fall deep into the ocean of incredible emotions. There's a time and a place for that. This is the usual pathway towards dating. But this pathway is not mandatory, necessary, or practical for all intents and purposes. Helen Fisher, Ph.D. from the University of Colorado, writes in her book, *Why We Love: The Nature and Chemistry of Romantic Love* that it's "No wonder lovers talk all night or walk till dawn, write extravagant poetry and self-revealing emails, cross continents or oceans to hug for just a weekend, change lifestyles, even die for one another." That explains why people are willing to take such risks regarding their jobs, professions, and marriages.

Now prepare yourself for a shocking statement; this is a missed opportunity for everyone, but women in particular. Drenched in chemicals that bestow focus, stamina, and vigor, and driven by the brain's motivating engine, why not use this as a way to leverage your power and career?

It's time to stop denying sexuality and embrace the chemistry. We can activate it when we want, it's free and it's healthy! Sex is not the exclusive domain of men; we can gaze upon our lover (male or female) in all their equal parts. We can take this focus and energy and channel it into our business, projects, or anything we are working on professionally or personally. When you walk into that boardroom to make that presentation, you will crush it because that energy will radiate, and you'll be bursting with dopamine and motivation! You will be firing on all pistons, and you'll write that brilliant report at the speed of light, creativity will be abundant, you will have throngs of ideas", you'll be immensely productive! you'll be immensely productive! When you are continuously harnessing your sexual energy, it lasts. It's not that you have to go have intercourse and then quickly run to the meeting before the feeling goes away. In fact, you don't need to have intercourse at all; all the other parts of lusting, attraction and flirting are enough to trigger the state of mind.

What's more, if you are studious about it, with self-awareness and self-control, you can have the surrounding humans in your business drenched with this "giddy" and "irrational" behavior; thus, you can influence them, or impact them, in a positive way. As another facet of charm, get that contract signed. Win that negotiation. To be clear, this is not a manipulation tactic, it's just that everyone will be in a better "mood", a better state of mind.

While attraction and lust are mostly a domain exclusive to romantic encounters, some neurochemicals also facilitate attachment, strengthening friendships, parent-child bonding, social cohesion, and many other intimacies. The two primary hormones here appear to be oxytocin and vasopressin. Like dopamine, oxytocin, "the cuddle hormone," is produced by the hypothalamus and released in large quantities during sex, breastfeeding, and childbirth. That may seem like an extraordinary assortment of activities, but friendship and social encounters are critical here. Business is all about relationships, but doesn't always need to involve flirting and crushing. We certainly should be aware of the benefits of the chemicals that can form outstanding bonds and friendships in business too. People do business with those they know and those they trust. So find whatever bonding mechanism works for you. By the way, bonding by flirting, charming and crushing can be just as genuine as anything else. It's all about intention and consent.

Sex triggers the release of a lot of oxytocin, creating heaps of social trust for a period of time. Oxytocin creates feelings of attachment designed to lead to enduring commitment and a bonding mechanism that keeps couples together when they have children. Both sexes release oxytocin during orgasm and thereby promote bonding when adults are intimate. As the theory stands, the more sex a couple has, the stronger their bond is.

Then there's the downside. Vasopressin is another culprit chemical that facilitates the long-term commitment phase. High levels of vasopressin can lead to a decline in females' sexual motivation and can lead to feelings of neglect and even hostility toward a sexual partner. For males, vasopressin rears its head during arousal, can increase erectile response, and may be associated with increased urges to engage in sexual behavior. These two outcomes certainly sound in conflict with each other. We can't ignore these consequences and should be aware of them. What is of particular relevance here is how oxytocin, the so-called "love hormone," also has a dark side to it, associated with jealousy, envy, erratic behavior, suspicion, and irrationality, along with a host of other less-than-positive emotions and moods. Things are rarely as simple as they may seem; dopamine is also controlling both the good and the bad. We experience surges of dopamine for our virtues and our vices, closely related to addiction, for example. The same brain regions that are activated when we're feeling attraction light up when drug addicts take cocaine and when we binge eat sweets. In a way, attraction mimics the same feelings and responses as an addiction, but for a human being rather than for a substance. A little self-control is required here. Too much of anything is rarely good.

Similarly, the same brain regions are activated when we become addicted to material goods (shopping addiction!), and one can go into "withdrawal." At the same time elevated oxytocin can also fuel prejudice and, taken to the extreme, can cause people to act wildly and recklessly. Thus, like dopamine, oxytocin can be a bit of a double-edged sword. Let's get around to an important point. Sexual arousal (but not necessarily attachment) appears to turn off regions in our brain that regulate critical thinking, self-awareness, and rational behavior, including parts of the prefrontal cortex. Again, this helps to explain some workplace sexual entanglements and infidelity to a certain extent.

There are other factors to a relationship gone sour; neglect, growing apart, poor communication. Still, these are more pre-cursors that lay the foundation for a potential shift in thinking, when someone becomes open to infidelity. If we are in the workplace or a business situation and find ourselves attracted to someone, how much of our decision to "cross the line" (assuming we are in a monogamous relationship) and take it past flirting comes down to biology? We can draw some connections to the dark side of oxytocin and dopamine to false accusations in harassment cases. It can explain how a once 'consensual' relationship/encounter turns into something else, perhaps when each person is at a different stage, chemically speaking. Someone feels hurt, jealous, irrational. Then we've got a workplace harassment claim on our hands. Not to say that's how they all go, just saying this is one of many possible scenarios. What helps here is awareness and understanding of personal limits. Some of these situations could be avoided if more people understood their neurochemicals.

When it comes to love, are we at the mercy of our biochemistry? Theoretically, if our hormones determine all of this, you'd think we could have some sort of "chemistry" with everyone. But whether or not it goes further is still up to you. Chemicals play a vital role, but I don't think it is deterministic, as some may believe. There is always agency. Falling in love, being in love, crushing on someone, stimulates all of your happy chemicals at once. That's why it feels so amazing. Our brain evolved to activate reproduction. Humans are not made to sustain the "feel good" emotions all the time. There is some down time needed. From a sex-positive approach, those who make an effort can have meaningful and mindful sexual relationships. That should be highly encouraged for mature adults, who take responsibility for their actions and have high self-awareness levels. This process is not for the faint of heart, but when we understand our happy chemicals, we can leverage them in our career and business and relationships, concurrently or simultaneously.

Let's dig into this just a bit deeper so we can all understand what the heck is happening in our bedrooms and the office! Are you sitting down? If so, stand up so you can feel the shock and awe; women need twice as much sex as men. Insert horny happy face here. According to Health Expert Dr. Stephanie Estima in her article *Why Women Need Twice As Much Sex As Men*, data suggests two to three times a week minimum. Women need twice as much positive reinforcement externally than men to derive the same motivation in dopamine activity. We can blame biology here. In any case, all the creativity, strategy, and amazing things in our brain light up when we have regular sex. More energy, more productivity, more everything. When we look at reasons people divorce or split, it's often related to communication issues, financial issues, or libido differences. A ton of research demonstrates the strong biological drive behind men's desire, but there is also some compelling evidence to explain why women need to be having more sex. In most relationships, there isn't necessarily a lack of talking; it's more than just men and women "not understanding each other". That phrase (and book) *Men are from Mars and Women are from Venus* has been kicking around for decades. Referring back to the science behind it, let's contextualize it.

Our left and right brain functions differently. Our brain's left side is very mechanical and highly task-oriented, strategic, mathematical, and thought to be linear. The left is where a neurotransmitter called dopamine originates and where our motivation derives. When we feel great because we've accomplished something, a micro-goal perhaps, or someone likes our post on Instagram, that's a dopamine hit. And, we are likely to repeat these behaviors because they feel good. When we are highly motivated, we can stay engaged, passionate, and on task. What is super cool, too, we can increase and stimulate our dopamine. Try music! ... but not junk food (too addictive and harmful results). Studies show that listening to our favourite music has a similar effect on our brains as other pleasure-inducing activities like having sex! MRI and PET scans reveal that when we listen to music that excites us, our brain releases dopamine during the most exciting moments of the song and even in anticipation of those moments. That's just one of several methods to induce healthy amounts of dopamine.

The right side of our brain tends to be more sensual. It's more creative. It's emotional. It's passion. This is where serotonin originates, our happiness hormone. Interesting point, and key to the story, you can't raise your own serotonin levels. (unlike dopamine) Boohoo! Someone has to do it for you.

Serotonin is only deployed from external stimuli such as positive feedback from our friends, family, lovers, colleagues, and our environment. Serotonin levels also increase dopamine levels. If we are receiving positive feedback from our partner, like moaning and screaming and displaying sexual ecstasy (just as an example), we are usually motivated to continue in the activity. In the context of our relationship or sex, our partner raises our serotonin levels, which in turn increases our dopamine. Another kicker: men have double the serotonin receptors as women. Therefore, it is argued that women need twice as much love and affection to achieve similar happiness levels as men or to have the same levels of serotonin and dopamine. I guess that's the exchange for the disproportionate amount of over 8,000 nerve endings in the clitoris, double that of the entire penis.

Whether you're dating or in a relationship, remember the serotonin – dopamine relationship and the differences between men and women. For the women in your life, your partner, or your co-worker, she may benefit from more positive reinforcement than the men. Don't get it wrong; men need their levels of acknowledgment, just differently. The men around you require appreciation to continue to be motivated while also feeling respected. At the end of the day, we all benefit from being appreciated and recognized. The downside is that some things can get complicated, especially in workplace and business relationships or affairs. In the least of situations, the wrong kind of appreciation and recognition can create tension in the workplace or during business proceedings, now more than ever in a post #metoo era. One must exercise the capacity for good judgment, respect, and boundaries. Some people are ok with flirting, friendly touching, compliments, etc. Others are not. For both men and women. You have to feel them out. The framework of Sexual Intelligence in Business can help you through this.

FLOW STATE

Have you ever felt so immersed in an activity or project that you kind of lost track of time and were super productive? Some athletes refer to that state as "runners high". You may be experiencing the delightful and productive mental state that psychologists refer to as the Flow State. When you are truly living in the moment, entirely absorbed in the present activity, time flies, and you don't notice.

According to positive psychologist Mihály Csíkszentmihályi, that state is one of experiencing flow, a state of mind of deep immersion. The ego falls away (not the everyday use of the term ego is synonymous with arrogance, but the Freudian Concept of ego/id/superego consciousness)—time flies. Every action, movement, thought, activity, and decision flow without resistance, without doubt, using your brain and your skills 10x.

Flow is experienced in different ways by different people. You might experience flow while engaging in sports; many extreme sports athletes tap into this state of mind to achieve the absolutely incredible and record breaking results they do. The activity itself is not the ultimate determinator, but the engagement, deep immersion, and focus. I would be remiss not to mention the New York Times bestselling author and an award-winning journalist, and Executive Director of the Flow Research Collective, Steven Kotler, who has written extensively about the Flow State, all inspired by Csíkszentmihályi.

According to Csíkszentmihályi, ten factors (triggers) accompany the experience of flow. You don't need all of them at once, but as many as possible to get the best effect:

- Clear goals that are challenging but achievable
- The intense concentration and focused attention
- An intrinsically rewarding activity
- Knowing that the task is feasible, but still hard, a balance between skill level and the challenge. You will experience feelings of serenity; a loss of feelings of self-consciousness
- You will experience timelessness; a distorted sense of time; feeling so focused on the present that you lose track of time passing
- You are somehow getting immediate feedback (think about moaning or dirty talk during sex, for example)
- You will experience feelings of personal control over the situation and the outcome
- You will experience a lack of awareness of physical needs
- You will experience a complete focus on the activity itself

How to Achieve Flow

So what can you do to increase your chances of achieving flow? In his book *Flow: The Psychology of Optimal Experience,* Csíkszentmihályi explains that flow is likely to occur when someone faces a task with clear goals that require specific responses.

- To help induce a state of flow:
- You have a specific goal and plan of action

- It is an activity that you enjoy or passionate about
- There is an element of challenge
- You can stretch your current skill level

"Flow also happens when a person's skills are fully involved in overcoming a challenge that is just about manageable, so it acts as a magnet for learning new skills and increasing challenges," Csíkszentmihályi explains. "If challenges are too low, one gets back to flow by increasing them. If challenges are too great, one can return to the flow state by learning new skills."

There are practical applications of a flow state, most relevant here is in business and the workplace. One of his critical concepts is his theory is related to slightly extending oneself beyond one's current ability level. This slight stretching of one's existing skills can help the individual experience flow. You are punching above your weight, challenging yourself, pushing into areas that are a bit uncomfortable. You can take on that big project, apply for that job when you only have 4/10 of the requirements, go for that big deal, hit up that critical client, shoot for the stars!

The flow state has many advantages, such as improved performance, accelerated learning, rapidly increasing the mastery of a particular skill, and enhanced creativity. And guess what? Engaging in sex, crushing, flirting, with all its accompanying neurochemicals, can induce a flow state. Adam

Safron, a neuroscientist at Northwestern University, reviewed related studies and literature. In his article *Getting into the flow: Sexual pleasure is a kind of trance*, he writes "The idea that sexual experiences can be like trance states is, in some ways, ancient. It turns out modern understandings of neuroscience support this idea. [...] In theory, this could change the way people view their sexuality. Sex is a source of pleasurable sensations and emotional connection, but beyond that, it's an altered state of consciousness."

Like everything, there's a good side and a bad side. But when you find that balance, you'll see exponential results! When we better understand how the brain works and what motivates our behaviors, and how to channel that to our benefit, we can be monumentally more successful in our business, career and many other endeavors.

CHAPTER 9
FEMME FATALE VICE OR VIRTUE

There is something that I've been noticing over the years, and that has been concretized since I started doing research for this book in 2018: there appears to be a systemic effort in repressing sexual expression, most effectively towards women. The onus seems to be on women, to cover up, remove themselves from spaces, eliminate their sexuality in order to help men not be manipulated, to ensure that men to not lose control so as to not invite sexual harassment or worse, rape. We all seem to have bought into this paradigm of blaming women for their sexuality and blaming men for their sexual urges. What is worse, once people buy into this paradigm, they literally start to play out those roles because part of the human brain is strongly attracted to consistency. Even when the origins premise is wrong. According to Robert Cialdini's book on Influence, the Psychology of Persuasion, we as humans will continue in the name of remaining consistent. In this chapter, I'm going to open up a can of whoop ASS on this concept!

Femme Fatale

The femme fatale. A seductive woman who lures men into dangerous or compromising situations. A woman who attracts men by an aura of charm and mystery. The literal translation, disastrous woman.

This is a purity issue dressed up differently.

We can conjure those images in our minds of the characters in films, of the female sexual succubus manipulating men with their lustrous ways, convincing them to do things they would never otherwise consider. There is a paradox breathing down the neck of the femme fatale archetype, the sexist version of a cold and calculating creature versus the empowered woman, who embraces her sexuality and uses it to pursue her own goals. Again, manipulating for evil versus influencing for good.

When researching the term "real-life femme fatales", I ran into some fairly indicative stories. Most of the women that I could find were women that were reported as simply female murderers. Most of which are not beautiful at all. Yes, these women killed men. But there was nothing reported in their cases that they sexually lured their victims. Murder in the first degree, standardly criminal, if I could say such a thing, kind of way. They were not dressed sexually with red lipstick and a cigarette in their hands nor were they wearing corsets and high heels during their criminal acts. So why does sex get wrapped up in this when it has nothing to do with it at all?

There are several other accounts of actual women in history being labeled as femme fatales, except it appears that there was very little sexual manipulation of men explicitly, it was more assumed that they did. God forbid a woman get anywhere on her own accord. Cleopatra, Wu Zeitan, Harriette Wilson, Agnes Sorel, and Eva Perón for example, amongst several others, were women who frankly, stepped outside of the silent woman, mother of her children, housewife role. That is all it took to gain the label. Using her intellect, her leadership skills, her business savvy, or partaking in mutually consenting affairs, all were good enough criteria. Oh, and she might be pretty, might have nice boobs too. This stands to reason, and based on those criteria, all women are femme fatales.

In history, we have Eve, who convinced Adam to eat the fruit from the tree of knowledge and circumvent God's wishes and other mythological figures and fictional characters such as Medusa, Circe and Sirens. The Greek philosopher Socrates is said to have warned that a beauty's kiss was deadlier than a spider's venom. "What do you think you would suffer after kissing someone beautiful? Would you not immediately be a slave rather than free?" asked Socrates. "I counsel you . . . whenever you see someone beautiful, to flee without looking back."

This portrait of the femme fatale solely exists in Hollywood, in the arts, in the media and in minds of those who want to bring women down.

Dr. Catherine O'Rawe of Bristol University is the editor of an academic survey of the subject, Femme Fatale: Images, Histories, Contexts, and she notes that such fictional seductresses reflect society's trepidation towards independent women and "What's striking is that these figures [in Hollywood films] arose at the same time as concerns about emancipated women occupying the public sphere."

Professor Mark Jancovich, the co-author of Defining Cult Movies, writes "There was a feminist argument that the femme fatale was an attempt to demonise the independent working woman of the war years. [...] "She has been seen as part of the propaganda designed to push women out of men's jobs and back into the home. And Dr. Ellen Wright, from the University of East Anglia says "I see her as an incredibly powerful and wily character who not only drives the narrative, revels in her sexuality and looks utterly fabulous, but who ultimately sees the system for what it is and absolutely refuses to accept her place within it. Whether or not she is punished for her actions – and let's face it, she invariably is – I still think she carries a hugely empowering, invigorating message."

Surprise, surprise! There is no male equivalent. Oh wait, Homme Fatale! A quick search reveals, well, next to nothing. One movie, one book, and a pathetic attempt to retrofit the term to some Hollywood films of yesteryear. There really is no equivalent. Why? Are men not sexy? Have men not coerced women into sexual encounters? Ever? I'm being facetious obviously, but this is quite irritating.

Sexual Repression disguised as Piety and Modesty

This is a majorly sensitive topic, hotly debated and extremely nuanced. I'm not going to make any statements or conclusions about whether covering is good or bad, nor will I attempt to discuss here all of the many reasons, basis, or justifications for covering. It is said that in several religions, women cover or wear a veil as a way of curbing male sexual desire. In its traditional form, it is worn for several piety reasons, for both Christian and Muslims, but also for women to remain private and maintain modesty amongst unrelated males. There is a longstanding debate about whether Christians (and nuns specifically) cover for modesty, and there's a passage in the Bible that alludes to this. Some Jewish sects also practice forms of covering as part of the modesty-related dress standard called tzniut. Traditional sarees worn by Indian women symbolize modesty and humility.

Out of respect, I'm trying to be very careful here. The purpose of mentioning women covering any parts of their body is to demonstrate that this practice exists, across the globe, over millennia, cross-culturally, and amongst a multitude of religions. All that to say, women covering their bodies (or parts thereof) is ubiquitous. Many times for the purpose of honoring their God. But It seems women must cover to reduce the male gaze. It seems that it is the woman who must cover, because if she doesn't, she is the opposite of modest. This would make the woman obscene, indecent and vulgar. Just look up online all the synonyms. In the west, if she wears a short skirt and consumes alcohol at the party, she's asking to be raped. If she shows cleavage at the office, she's dressed inappropriately. Women must take up the suit, button-up real high, and in practicality, make yourself androgynous. Now, I'm not saying that everyone should walk around naked and wear bikini's at the office. The point here, again, the onus is on the woman. And it shouldn't be.

Just because she is sexy or beautiful, does not mean she is manipulative. People who are manipulative are likely going to be manipulators whether they are using sex or not. Women should be able to wear what is comfortable to them, that reflects their personality if they wish to do so, wear a suit if that makes them feel powerful, or wear runners because their feet hurt. The outfit women chose to wear should not be based on whether they will attract sexual harassment or not. This, in my view, is a tacit form of sexual repression of women. Maybe instead of burning bras, we should all go into work one day, with only our bra. That might make a stir.

At this point, it should come as no surprise that I am a proponent of dressing for success. Does that mean people need to dress sexy to be successful? If we could fully define what it means to dress sexy for everyone, we'd probably solve a lot of problems. This is for you to decide. Whatever makes you feel good.

I hope this short chapter has dispelled this false notion that women are naturally sexual manipulators and that men are these mindless creatures who can be put under a spell. These types of ideas do not serve humanity well.

CHAPTER 10

LOOKS MATTER ESPECIALLY IN BUSINESS

Looks Matter Especially In Business

When New Year's rolls around, losing weight tops the list of resolutions. Sometimes this can be for health reasons, but often, it's for appearances. Why are we concerned with body image? We have beliefs based on preconceived notions about ideal body weight, influenced by society, magazines, and media. Is that the full story? Or are there biological reasons at play here? And how will this help us in business?

In most cases, those who strive towards ultra-skinny or zero percent body fat are not always the healthiest individuals. There are several trigger points throughout time and space that motivate us to do the right or healthy thing such as exercise, quit smoking, eat vegan, live minimally, green smoothies, meditate, and so on. Of course, all of these things are intrinsically good, but it's often our desire to look better or appear beautiful that motivates us. Now, we may not like to admit to ourselves, never mind others, that we are inclined to look gorgeous. It's easier to believe it's for our health because otherwise, we fear being judged as vain. Whatever the intention, it's always useful to be healthier, but the bottom line is that everyone wants to look good. Paul Campos, Professor of Law at the University of Colorado, Boulder, and author of The Obesity Myth: Why America's Obsession With Weight Is Hazardous to Your Health" writes in a 2013 Op-Ed piece in the New York times that, "Americans have become increasingly obsessed with the supposed desirability of thinness, as thinness has become both a marker for upper-class status and a reflection of beauty ideals that bring a kind of privilege." Interesting note, it used to be a sign of poverty. Whereas if you were nicely plump, it meant you had enough fortune and resources to eat. A personal disclaimer here, I like to look good as much as the next person and I most certainly want a fit body to boot. But I do not endorse ultra-thinness, waif-like body shapes as some type of ideal. There are indeed some humans who are petit by nature and this is perfectly fine. Nor do I endorse extreme bodybuilding, taking hormones or muscles enhancements etc that are risks to health. The purpose here is to be healthy and optimize the body shape and frame that nature intended for you and that you feel comfortable in.

The belief that beauty or attractiveness, as subjective as they are, can give you an advantage is not entirely incorrect. This concept is a potent marketing tool used in social media and advertising, the fashion industry, printed media, the entire cosmetic surgery, and the beauty industry. But there is also research that suggests it can give us an advantage. According to Sociologist and writer, Heather Laine Talley in her 2016 Huffpost article, "It's not surprising that we are fixated on looks. Our appearance can positively and negatively affect us. Beautiful individuals make more money, earn higher grades, and are convicted at lower rates. Of course, the flip side is the costs that come with being perceived as ugly." Schneider et al., 2012 talks about how unattractive people are statistically mistreated, stating that preventing job advancement and worse is even considered more capable of engaging in criminal behavior.

These beliefs and perceptions lead us towards something called The Halo Effect. This type of cognitive bias surmises that our impressions of a person's appearance influence how we think and feel about their overall character. The initial impressions impact your evaluations of other traits and skills, which inevitably spills over to how people perceive you/them in many different aspects. The human brain is powerful and complex, and we all hold some degree of cognitive biases. For example, people perceived as attractive, successful, or likable are also seen as intelligent, kind, and funny, regardless of the factual evidence. Psychologist Edward Thorndike first coined the term the Halo Effect, in a 1920 paper titled The Constant Error in Psychological Ratings. He conducted a study that demonstrated that military personnel who were identified as attractive were correlated with characteristics such as leadership, physical appearance, intelligence, loyalty, and dependability.

There is research that shows how better-looking candidates fared better in elections. In 2013 White, Kenrick and Neuberg published a study, Beauty at the Ballot Box: Disease Threats Predict Preferences for Physically Attractive Leaders, which asks when and why voters prefer more attractive politicians? It has often been thought and often remains the case that it boils down to the halo effect. But they argue in a recent article in the journal Psychological Science, "people's preferences may be linked to historical adaptations for avoiding disease." The preference for pretty politicians seems to correlate with voters' concerns about germs because "past research has found that some of the features associated with beauty — smooth skin, shiny hair, body, and facial symmetry — are actually indicators of health."

Thinking about the adage, Look Good Feel Good, Mobius and Rosenblat write in their 2005 paper Why Beauty Matters, wrote that "Preferential treatment in return builds confidence as well as social and communication skills." If a person looks good, that person is treated better. When you are treated better, you play better in sports; apparently, you're a better teacher, a better student, the list goes on. That confidence, the literature suggests, translates into academic achievement and professional success. Based on this evidence, it stands to reason that if you can generate confidence, then you'll perform better too, looks notwithstanding.

Our appearance is a component of who we are, and one should take advantage of strengths, talents, and skills, in all their wonderful forms. It is curious that we venerate and respect characteristics like athletic ability, intelligence, genius, business acumen, and charisma. Yet, we associate beauty with vanity. If we "use" it, we should feel shameful, in fact, manipulative.

Physical attractiveness comes with benefits, obviously, and not only free drinks at bars. But benefits also come to those with Nobel Prizes, Olympic Gold Medals, and sending our rocket ships to space. Display of beauty is a widely used attraction method within nature. We choose and admire flowers, landscapes, art, architecture because of their beauty. But why not humans?

The fact is that appearance matters—optics matter. How you present yourself, present your products, and your business; these all matter, physically and creatively. Beauty and ascetics matter; for people, and it matters for products too. Let's look at marketing, such as packaging and commercials selling a lifestyle; if you drink this beer, you'll get chicks. If you purchase this makeup, you'll look beautiful. We buy into this, literally. People want to dine in chic restaurants, stay in upscale hotels.

We like to hear that looks don't matter, out of sensitivity. Some say that looks should not matter and that we should judge people's character by their actions, which is true. But as the research shows, people start identifying with beauty from the beginning of life. A person's character or behavior is ultimately measured by what they do, by their values, intellect, actions, and things they say. But looks are used as initial assessments, the brain categorizes and differentiates. Judging people by their appearance is a convenient, albeit sometimes ineffective tool. But it's quicker. It's easier. The brain likes that. In most cases, you never have that opportunity to get to know someone deeper. So we rely on "judge a book by its cover" when that's all we have time for. So we have a problem here that doesn't seem solvable in an obvious way.

Researchers have studied babies and how they react to appearances. For sure, adults are sensitive to physical differences; our brains are hardwired to categorize. Researchers Quinn, Slater, et al., in their Developmental Science Journal article, show a preference for attractive faces in human infants extends beyond conspecifics, tested newborns and young infants on their visual preferences. As soon as they get up to three months, they start to prefer their ethnicity; this suggests that visual preferences are learned by exposure. Not only do newborns prefer (meaning they looked longer) their mother's face over a stranger's, but they also have a propensity for attractive vs unattractive faces. One of the conclusions of the study is that babies like to gaze upon beautiful faces, as they spent more time fixated on attractive faces. "Attractiveness is not in the eye of the beholder, it's innate to a newborn infant," says Slater. "In a baby's mind, those beautiful faces may represent the stereotypical human face...which they have evolved to recognize." They further reinforce the notion that attractive faces are biological indicators that differentiates humans from other mammals.

When it comes to evolutionary psychology, there are a few indications that women's more prominent physical attractiveness is an evolutionary adaptation. Women have a broad range of socially acceptable options to enhance their beauty. Breasts, hip-to-waist ratios, hair length, jewelry, makeup, and products that promote youthfulness help to serve as signals and traits that are highly sought-after features, by both men and women! Generally speaking, people perceive women as the more beautiful of the genders, supporting the view that this is perhaps natural selection. This cognitive error likely has evolutionary roots, because generally, there is a preference for attractive qualities when choosing a mate, reasons for fertility, as it relates to evolutionary biology.

In 2018, Nigel Barber Ph.D., wrote Why Looks Still Matter as Women Gain Power, stating "Darwin recognized that some species evolve traits that enhance their attractiveness to potential mates. This generally affects the male genders in the animal world but, for our species, females are clearly the more ornamented sex based on their greater perceived attractiveness. Some aspects of esthetics may be baked into the brain before birth." Most men are far more concerned (and biologically programmed) with achieving intercourse. These days, they don't care about fake eyelashes or which jeans women are wearing.

In 2016, in her Guardian article, Lisa Hilton, *Time to be grown-up about female desire*, writes about the female gaze and how women do, in fact, judge males by their appearances but are reluctant to admit. We do speak about penis size between us girls. Amongst a whole bunch of other things related to looks. Lisa Hilton writes, "Women are vicious about other women. A whole industry is run, if not controlled, by women whose aim is to make other women feel insecure, so they buy more stuff. Naomi Wolf's contention that the beauty industry reflects a sublimation of the male gaze imposed by patriarchy doesn't quite ring true when confronted with the acres of gleeful newsprint devoted to J-Lo or Gwyneth Paltrow looking less than perfect. Women may sneer at men's looks in private, but in public, we're still happy to let them strut - and work off our frustration by criticising celebrities we still spend fortunes trying to emulate....If women were prepared to be more honest about the critical objects of their own gaze, they might waste less time bitching about each other."

In the Business and the Workplace

There are several ways that the halo effect can influence people's perceptions of others in business and work settings. The halo effect ignites biases affecting performance reviews. An employee, client, or business associate's positive attitude and enthusiasm may overshadow their shortcomings, thereby obtaining better reviews, making more sales, and negotiating better deals.

In many cases, physical attractiveness boosts a person's self-confidence, but it also affects their income and financial situation. A 2015 study published in the Journal of Economic Psychology, by Matt Parrett titled *Beauty and the Feast: Examining the Effect of Beauty on Earnings Using Restaurant Tipping Data* discovered that, on average, attractive food servers earned approximately $1,261 more per year in tips than counterparts. Beautiful people tend to get higher salary offers, more frequent promotions, and close more business deals. The halo effect impacts job applicants, as employers consider applicants who are more attractive as likable and subsequently regard them as smarter, more competent, or even better qualified. A few studies on how much makeup a woman uses affects how women are treated at work and business. Nancy Etcoff, author of "Survival of the Prettiest" and researcher from Harvard who published (along with colleagues Stock, Haley, Vickery, and House) "Cosmetics as a Feature of the Extended Human Phenotype: Modulation of the Perception of Biologically Important Facial Signals". It shows results that compared women who wore makeup versus non-makeup wearers and concluded that people view a groomed female as more attractive, competent, likable, and trustworthy. But too much makeup could be viewed as untrustworthy and manipulative. Daniel Hamermesh, the author of "Beauty Pays" (Princeton University Press, 2011), indicates beautiful people get a "leg up." Makeup can make women appear more likable because we think that people who care to take care of themselves are more likely to care for I don't think its much of a stretch then, to say that women also like men who are nicely groomed and appear to take care of themselves.

In their 2004 study, Brase and Richmond revealed that what you wear positively affects people and yourself. They evaluated attire in doctor-patient interactions and discovered how clothes or outfits, like lab coats, are associated with authority. We've all felt this before, with the Look-Good-Feel-Good effect. You put on that power suit and BAM! you instantly feel good. When you feel good, you'll project confidence. It's a positive feedback loop. Slepian et al. in 2015, in their study *The Cognitive Consequences of Formal Clothing*, in the Journal of Social and Personality Psychology Science, found that "putting on formal clothes makes us feel powerful, and that changes the basic way we see the world."

The truth is, thought most of us are average. Not only are people in magazines highly photoshopped, but most of the "beautiful" people we see in the media have the money and resources to keep up a particular appearance. The percentage of extremely beautiful people by certain social standards in the world is relatively low. So low in numbers, they are not much to worry about on a day to day basis. The thing to worry about is social comparison bias, where we dislike those that are "better" than us and compare ourselves to unrealistic measures. And from that, are we making policies and creating societal values based on the few or the many? In any case, there's always going to be someone better than us, smarter than us, more prominent than us. The question is, how much and in what ways are we going to let that affect us?

As women gain more power and equity, we may think they would start to be less concerned about physical attractiveness. And yet, their economic spending on fashion, cosmetics, cosmetic surgery, and beauty treatments increases. This is why power and choices matter. It is essential to take your physical appearance seriously, in one way or another. Let's ask ourselves why we get up in the morning and get ready. Yes, there are necessary hygiene activities (and thank goodness for that!), but why do we try so hard to look fashionable, professional, or sexy, and why do we try to identify with a particular "look" or "style"? Why do so many of us do our hair and makeup and shave and spend tons of money on beauty and aesthetics?

How much do looks matter? Let's look at a few statistics, shall we?

- Plastic Surgery industry net worth over $20 Billion
- Beauty Industry net worth at 445 billion
- Fashion Industry 2.4 Trillion!!

Consumers have power. In the last ten years, we've seen a significant increase in beauty lines, beauty regimes, more anti-aging products, eyelash extensions, the waxing, the makeup tattooing, the nails, the social media makeup influencers! It's exploding. So what does that tell us?

It's worth repeating; some people have a natural-born advantage such as intelligence, genius, creativity, athletic ability. At the same time, many people work very hard and develop these attributes. We celebrate those characteristics and qualities. But if someone is born with beauty or overt sexuality, society suggests that they suppress it, and we chastise it, we shame them. We are happy to put them on magazines and ads to look at, but how dare they claim respect for their beauty. This doesn't seem right. If that's your superpower, then it's your choice to foster it.

Appearance varies, and some of those differences make us uncomfortable. Own that discomfort. It's the essential first step to pushing through it. Then, do the work of unpacking your stereotypes and biases, because we all have them. Our judgments towards others may reveal more about what we think of ourselves. Carl Jung eloquently put it into words: "Everything that irritates us about others can lead us to an understanding of ourselves."

It's been my experience that looks or beauty may get your foot in the door, but it's ultimately intellect, ideas, and delivering results that lead to success. As mentioned above, the belief that beauty or attractiveness, as subjective as they are, can offer an advantage is not entirely incorrect but it's not correct either. There is a significant amount of research that suggests that beauty and attractiveness can offer an advantage. But beauty and attractiveness are very subjective, which is great because everyone has different preferences, IS in the eye of the beholder, meaning, there's more to beauty and attractiveness than what the magazines try to sell us. You do not have to be ultra skinny, you do not have to wear tons of makeup and have huge fake lashes or constantly be buying up the latest fashion trends. Taking care of yourself, being healthy, owning your body, letting your natural beauty and sexuality shine through. Respect yourself and do not feel shameful for presenting your most beautiful self.

CHAPTER 11
HARNESS EROTIC CAPITAL AND SEXUAL TRANSMUTATION

I'm going to reveal a little secret that I've been hinting at throughout the book. Ok, it's not much of a secret anymore. We have the ability to generate and harness our sexual energy and channel it towards our business, career, or other creative and intellectual endeavors. Runners high isn't just for athletes, magnificent works of art and genius inventions are not exclusive to a very special few, you can use your sexual energy and the Sexual Intelligence in Business framework to make transformational changes in your life and achieve your hopes, dreams and goals.

The Institute for the Study of Labor, an independent economic research institution in Germany, published their findings in The Effect of Sexual Activity on Wages by Dr. Nick Drydakis in 2013. They found that people ages 26-50 who engaged in sex four or more times a week earned 5 percent more in wages. If you have sex once a week, you may make 3.2 percent more than those with no sex. So don't tell me that sex and business don't go together! Drydakis goes on to conclude that "People need to love and be loved—sexually and non-sexually—by others. In the absence of these elements, many people become susceptible to loneliness, social anxiety, and depression that could affect their working life," and adds "Sexual activity is a key aspect of personal health and social welfare that influences individuals across their lifespan."

The same study analyzed data in which 7,500 men and women ages 18-65 were asked about their sexual activity, personal health history, and income. Researchers found that not only do people who have more sex earn higher wages, they're also less prone to health issues. We understand already from a previous chapter how this is occurring as related to neurochemicals. The sexual energy you experience and neurochemicals flowing provide a rich resource, full of untapped potential. The way in which you utilize this precious resource can enhance your life and career! Sexual transmutation may be the answer to harnessing your sexual energy to 10x your business!.

Napoleon Hill, the originator of the concept of sexual transmutation, wrote a fascinating book on personal development called *Think and Grow Rich*. A quick caveat, it was 1937, and it is clear that he wrote the book for men. Nevertheless, the concepts remain interesting and can be applied to everyone. Given the "times," I intend on forgiving the man for his "reptilian brain" as it were. Napoleon Hill said, "Sex desire is the most powerful of human desires. When driven by this desire, men can develop keenness of imagination, courage, will-power, persistence, and creative ability unknown to them at other times." The early signs of 'flow state' it seems. I can say from personal experience, he's definitely on to something here.

In his book, Hill refers to accounts from the wealthiest and most successful men in the US in the 1930s, how they have remarkably high sex drives, and attributes their outstanding achievement to having "learned the art of sex transmutation". He's not saying to abstain from sex altogether, but rather he discusses how to channel the sexual energy, how we can harness our sexual power, transmute it, and use it to fuel our endeavors in the world of business and life success. As a caveat, Hill seemed to be delusional in his sense of grandeur and most of the claims of his association with successful historical figures and institutions have been either refuted or are unsubstantiated. He had tons of business failures, but you've got to give him credit, this guy kept going! The ultimate entrepreneur, a tiny bit crazy, a hustler by definition who did not let his failures stop him. Nevertheless, when we look at his list of book titles, we can clearly see the foundations of the self-help book industry, for which he does receive credit.

Napoleon Hill got many things wrong, but a few things right. But so did Freud. He noted that "Love is the emotion, which serves as a safety valve, and insures balance, poise and constructive effort. Love, romance, and sex may lift one to an altitude of a genius." Laura Garnet, performance strategist and author of The Genius Habit, says, "Sex and love combined are the secret sauce. Like any pleasurable activity, if you are not in love with yourself and fully engaged with it, you will not see as much benefit. It's just like doing a workout but beating yourself up mentally while doing it: your negative mental chatter will negate the workout benefits. The same goes for sex. Great, connected, passionate sex can be the fuel you are looking for that next big idea or inspiration you need to go to the next level in your career."

Sex can be associated with achievement, but there is a lack of discussion about this, particularly among women. There are very few prominent public examples of women using their sexual energy professionally and successfully. At least to what they are willing to admit. And if there were, it seems as those women are preconditioned to reject those examples of something worth respecting. We see plenty of people using sex in the wrong, harmful (and illegal) way, but its curious why people are afraid to demonstrate positive examples when there is so much to gain from that. Unfortunately, something that has come out of the metoo movement is the notion that everyone, and in particular women, must subdue and hide their sexuality, for their own protection. I understand why people feel that way, but I don't think it's the answer. Instead, let's take this opportunity to explore other aspects that can make us more successful in business and in our careers.

How to use Sexual Transmutation?

There are methods to which you can induce some personal arousal. When you feel horny, aroused or your juices are flowing, feel the intensity of those neurochemicals and try fueling that energy. Fantasies can be helpful, so can flirting, but once you're "there" you better write a damn business plan, make some art, trade some stocks and shares, learn a language or read a complex science paper. Tap that!

Seriously though, there are some technical aspects to this. Ruwan Meepagala, certified orgasm coach, gives a few tips on his blog on *How to Channel Sex Energy to Fascinate, Attract Abundance, and Create Your Reality*. He outlines transmutation as changing a "lower" form of energy into a "higher" form. Connecting it to the Law of Attraction, which many people have started referring to in different permutations, especially since the book The Secret came out. Honestly, I think just being aware of the possibility is half the battle. It is like stopping to smell the roses. We often just run by them, but when we take that second, stop and savor the gorgeous scent that flowers emit, then we appreciate the sensation. Or like floating in water, we can float, when we get in the right position and intention, with otherwise, you just sink down.

Hill states, "when harnessed and redirected along other lines, this motivating force maintains all of its attributes and keenness of imagination, courage...which may be used as powerful creative forces". It's much more than merely thinking positively; there is some science behind this. Taking into account *mindful sex* (which is the practice of mindfulness applied during sex), getting in touch and present with our mind and our emotions is the first place to start. When we are in alignment with the universe, we are rewarded with abundance. Instead of creating life, we create other things for the intrinsic benefit itself. Then the universe endows us in return.

This may all seem very esoteric. But there's so much written about this, and it goes way back in history. Currently, when we sense sexual energy as a feeling, we associate it with sex. Arousal, pleasure, and anticipation are the big examples of those feelings. We can actually convert those into energy, motivation, and tactile sensation. These are universal concepts found in many different models, including Chinese medicine, Ayurveda, western alchemy, most religions, yoga, mindfulness, and even Michael Chekhov's acting technique. We can also think about it like smiling. When we are upset, we can change our state of mind, even by forcing out a smile. The physical action creates the emotion. The emotion in return recreates physical sensations. Like a positive feedback loop.

One key factor in utilizing sexual transmutation is the ability to ground and stabilize the energy to channel it properly. It does not necessarily happen automatically, most notably because most people do not have that kind of intentional sex although they should try. We have to cultivate the sensations. Suppose you think about it as a lovely meal. It doesn't occur just when you buy the ingredients; you have to follow an intentional pathway and prepare before eating and enjoying it. If you have an open heart, the sensations will arise. That will poetically convert into attention, leading to ideas and creative associations. You cannot force transmutation. One cannot command their genitals to give them a million-dollar idea. One can only feel pleasure and be open to the possibility and then the intentions materialize effortlessly, but you have to pay attention. It's easiest to practice during sexual intercourse or self-pleasure; you can follow the physical sensations because they are strong. Once you have that down, you can see how you can evoke that when just flirting, or feeling a little bit attracted to someone, a crush, sexting, viewing sexual imagery, a fantasy in your mind. When you have the practice down, you can keep it going through triggers.

There are some schools of thought that say when a man ejaculates, he is losing his qi. Dr. Justin Lehmiller, in a 2018 Vice article, *We Looked into Whether Having Sex Affects Your Athletic Performance* postulates that since the days of the ancient Greeks and Romans, it's been a widely held belief among men that they should avoid sex before any sporting competition. "The no-sex-before-sports rule is rooted in a fear that sex will sap men of their testosterone and energy, thereby harming their athletic performance. Consistent with this idea, it's easy to find news reports about boxers, football players, MMA fighters, soccer players, and other athletes who abstain from sex (often at the urging of their coaches) during training or around major competitions, such as the Olympics and the World Cup." Can a pre-competition roll in the hay necessarily drain your strength? According to a study in The Journal of Sexual Medicine, "no sex before the competition" isn't based in reality.

In traditional Chinese culture, Qi or Ch'i is considered a vital energy force forming part of any living entity. Similar to the way eastern philosophies envision the chakras, in that they have a location or portal in the body. Qi translates as "air" and figuratively as "material energy", "life force", or "energy flow". Although Hill is not explicitly referring to Qi, I think he is talking about the same thing. That is why some coaches and athletes advocate abstaining from sexual intercourse before a big game or competition. I dug into this a bit, and there are a few studies with different albeit imperfect research methods. According to Zavorsky et al., in their article *Sexual Activity the Night Before Exercise Does Not Affect Various Measures of Physical Exercise Performance*, the overall results indicate there is no direct causation of a decrease in strength, "torque," or athletic performance of a man having intercourse the night before. Very limited research has been conducted with women athletes. There are limitations to focusing on strength as an outcome measure. It would be interesting to study other behavioral aspects.

The moral of the story? Have. More. Sex.

EROTIC CAPITAL

So now we know how to use sexual energy internally and physically to our benefit. Let's discuss another less profound concept and, for all intents and purposes, much more practical, tangible but also controversial. Understanding our erotic capital can provide us with benefits. Much like a currency and much like capitalism, this is not available to all, and one can expect some backlash from those who cannot or will not use their erotic capital. We need to be ready for that.

In *What is Gender Bias in the Workplace*, Bailey Reiners writes that "the glass ceiling is a metaphor for the evident but intangible hierarchical impediment that prevents minorities and women from achieving elevated professional success. Due to contributing factors, like the aforementioned types of bias, women and minorities experience a barrier that prevents them from reaching upper-level roles in leadership and the C-Suite." In reality, women experience thousands of microaggressions and must navigate disadvantages that men never consider. The *glass ceiling* is what's unavailable, or the things that are available to us at a price. For most, in business and the workplace, it permeates traditional, patriarchal, and masculine dominated sectors. So what to do? Turn it around and flip it on its head. Yes, things are changing, but it is still mostly a boys club. But we can play with that.

Since women are working within a flawed system, some choose to play by a boys club code to get ahead. All is fair in love and war. Sexuality can be a powerful tool for women in business, but we will hear that it is exploitative and anti-feminist to use it to our advantage. Beatrice Lockhard, in her article about erotic capital, asks, "to people who make judgments and proclamations, to whom is this behaviour exploitative? Because I know that I am using the more reptilian elements of my male colleagues' brains to advance in a way I might not be able to otherwise, and that, to me, feels like exploiting their weaknesses, not mine. I know what I'm doing, and why I'm doing it, and the fact that they are falling into it only makes them the victims, in my mind."

She also goes on to explain how men love to be flirted with and have their egos stroked. I would argue we all like that quite a bit. When someone gives us positive attention, we tend to be receptive to that. Everyone wants to feel like they are attractive and desired. Honing in on the important person in the room and charming them, can pay off. Yes, this point of view may seem extreme but if we can grease the wheels or smooth things over or build a bond with someone through sexual energy, if it feels right, then go for it.

Sociologist Dr. Catherine Hakim in her book called *Honey Money: The Power Of Erotic Capital,* suggests that knowing how to use our sexuality is critical to success at work and in business as intelligence, skill, and professional qualifications. Enter Sexual Intelligence in Business. Albert Einstein used his intelligence, Usain Bolt used his speed; Picasso used his creativity. We all have skills and abilities that are presumably natural-born or developed over time. "Good looks" and "sexual practice" have gotten a bad rap and for some reason are not respected in the same way. You don't need to be a supermodel to apply these methods, either. I know many men and women who are not traditionally "good looking" and certainly not supermodel gorgeous. Still, there's something about them that is so very attractive and makes me want to be around them! Charisma, attitude, humour, these things are sexy too!

According to Freud, we are sexual beings, and eroticism permeates every aspect of our consciousness. Erotic capital, intellectual capital, and athletic capital should be looked upon in the same way. Those who strongly resist are those who are uncomfortable with their sexuality and then transfer that onto others. What's more, many more women use erotic capital; they don't like admitting it possibly because they think it makes them look vain. In an article titled "I use my sex appeal to get ahead at work... and so does ANY woman with any sense", by Samantha Brick, a recent survey found that 87 percent of women would flirt with a male colleague if it meant they got their way. People like to be flattered, people like attention. Let's embrace that.

While you might think this is close to prostitution, Dr. Hakim says erotic capital has real value in the job market and refers to countless studies that back this up. While you don't need to sleep with anyone, you can dress in what "decision-makers appreciate." If one is to probe into stories from other women, we will find that women all do it to some extent or the other, but they fear judgment. Mostly from other women.

For example, Barbara Corcoran, real estate guru and an investor on ABC's Shark Tank, is a living and breathing example of using her erotic capital in a way that worked for her. She says "When I was building my business, I would walk into a room of 600 men in dark suits, and I dressed like a guy in a nice pants suit, no one would say hi to me no one would entertain me. The minute I started wearing bright suits and I would have a nice length skirt on, and I would just roll up the middle and walk into that room, everyone paid attention to me." We should never be reduced to their sexuality, there is obviously more to people than that. But it seems Barbara is doing pretty well for herself, so we may wish to consider her as an interesting example.

On the flip side, this strategy could backfire. You can't control other people's perceptions, and you can't predict their past experiences that inform the lens they look through in life. You have to read each situation and person and apply the right strategy that suits the circumstance. Relying solely on looks is not a universally successful tactic. Although this particular element is not something that men have to contend with, they have their issues to deal with, and they are at war with each other. It's as ruthless as you can imagine. Men and women have different pressures at work and in business, and nobody is escaping from challenges. Indeed, men face risks of tactics backfiring, but in different ways than women.

This reality may be horrific to some. Again, given the post #metoo era, it sounds contradictory right now, but sexual transmutation and erotic capital really can be an effective way to traverse the barriers. Sometimes, women are each other's worst enemies. For some feminists, it's a zero-sum game. If a woman harnesses her sexuality or femininity, it's at the sacrifice of professionalism and intellect. I would argue that the decision should lie with the individual and if it works for you, go for it. Some will disagree, and that's ok. But are we ready to shame women for this? If we map on the Sexual Intelligence in Business framework, there is room to gain the benefits and mitigate the risks.

You have to own the attitude. If you want to employ this technique and yield the results you are looking for, go right ahead. If not, then don't. But don't judge. We underestimate the ability of a man to refrain from being swayed by women's sexual energy, beauty, or femininity. We also underestimate their ability to appreciate those qualities AND STILL focus on what you are saying, your ideas, your work, and your results. Incidentally, men do the same. If a man is good looking, don't think he's not using his charm for one second. And why wouldn't he? There's nothing wrong with that, primarily if it works.

If you know your assets, it's not vain to use this to your advantage. Some women feel the need to create an alter ego to deal with the moral dilemma they face. They may laugh at jokes they don't find funny or listen to stories they don't give a shit about, just to appease their male superior. But I think everyone does a bit of that. Again, I'm not judging, do what you must do. The difference is to find a real way to connect with people so that you don't have to fake it. There is always something to like about everyone. There's still a common ground to find. When you genuinely care about people, instead of villainizing, victimizing, or objectifying, then it's effortless to find ways to build genuine relationships. When you use your erotic capital for good, then you'll enhance your business ten fold.

We cannot rely on rigid rules and regulations to structure everything in our lives. Dr. Camille Paglia, Author of Free Women, Free Men, Sex, says, "We have got to make women realize they are responsible, that sexuality is something that belongs to them. They have enormous power in their sexuality. It's up to them to use it correctly and be wise...". There is no single universal method, but the freedom for women to choose what works best for them and those choices need to be respected. A problem with 'women's empowerment' is how often women do the opposite of empowering each other. We need to be more respectful of the choices people make.

THE BEGINNING

The Anti-Climax

Normally, this would be the point in the book where we wrap up everything into a nice neat bow of a conclusion. But I'm not going to do that here. We tend to think of subjects in a very linear and vertical way, as evidenced by the way academic disciplines or business sectors are often organized. And this organizing principle makes sense, as we have previously discussed. It's easier on the brain. What we lack in many areas, is a systems-thinking approach. A holistic way of looking at things and linking ideas together. This is a good thing to do because everything is essentially connected, one way or the other. Such changes are indeed taking place in academia and business, but we're not there yet. Bringing together multiple stakeholders from different areas, disciplines, sectors, whatever you want to call them, to move ideas forward. Otherwise, you just stay stuck in your silo. Look at all these different topics covered in the book: history, consent, workplace, respect, #metoo, own your body, power, empathy, patriarchy, education, love, sexism, negotiation, looks, identity, emotions, altered states, communication, erotic capital, feminism, grey thinking, sexual transmutation. Most authors steer clear of tackling a multitude of topics, but rather choose to focus in and do the deep dive. Which is great. But at some point, someone has to connect the dots. This is what I'm trying to do. Not to solve all problems, but rather start to show you that all these things are related and conjoined, in a multitude of combinations. There is no conclusion here because this is just the beginning of the conversation. Now that researchers and other authors have tackled these topics in-depth, let's come back out of the rabbit hole and start discussing how to move forward.

We have not yet seen a world in which we have a diversity of leadership that can somehow transcend the parts of us that hold us back from greatness. My hope is that I've given readers another set of tools, Sexual Intelligence in Business, that you can add to your repertoire, that can help individuals and societies achieve their goals.

The whole reason I wrote this book, as you know, was my reaction to the #metoo movement. Not just the second-order consequences, but also to contribute to changing the narrative. I know many others share my thoughts that the #metoo narrative went in a direction that, at times, is a bit absolutist and it feels like we are all kind of painted into a corner. That doesn't feel good and it doesn't seem right. For sure that wasn't the intention. People are just afraid now, to say something. We may have the right to free speech, but many don't exercise this, not even at the basic levels. Being honest with ourselves, with our partners, our friends, family, co-workers, colleagues and clients. Nevermind, protesting, changing policy, impacting the world, reporting a rape. We must speak up. Everyone must speak up. With any luck, enough people will read this book and either be super-empowered or super pissed off. Any kind of reaction, I'll take it. To provoke the conversation.

So, if you are on the "I wanna be super-empowered" side of things, that's great! There are tons of books out there offering to help you from self-motivation, to get healthy, work hard, or the opposite messaging of slow down! Find your passion, or passion finds you. Marketing schemes and sales strategies, its all "out there". But what about, "in there"? You have everything you need, inside you, right now. Your sexual energy can be just the fuel you need, and if you apply the Sexual Intelligence in Business framework, throughout all the topics and locations discussed in the chapters, you will feel more empowered than ever.

My hope is that we can create a more sex-positive society, business, and work environment. I hope we can stop demonizing sex and realize all the great potential sex offers us, other than just reproduction. I would love to see Sexual Intelligence as a respected characteristic. This is beyond 'normalizing' and into full-on embracing, activating, utilizing, and witnessing

The Beginning

the crumbling of these restrictive systems and thought patterns that hold us back from being our true and best human selves.

Provoke Conversation - Empower Yourself - Enhance your Business

BIBLIOGRAPHY

CHAPTER 1

De Botton, A. (2016). Relationships. The School of Life. https://b-ok.cc/book/3400178/b372d4

Encyclopædia Britannica. (2016). Enlightenment. Encyclopædia Britannica Online, Encyclopædia Britannica Inc.

Hourly History. The Age of Enlightenment: A history from beginning to end: Chapter 3. https://web.archive.org/web/20170303123359/http://publishinghau5.com/The-Age-of-Enlightenment--A-History-From-Beginning-to-End-page-3.php

Hitchcock, T. (2012). The reformulation of sexual knowledge in eighteenth-century England. Signs, 37(4), 823-832. doi:10.1086/664467.

Sigler, D. (2015). Sexual enjoyment in British Romanticism: Gender and psychoanalysis. McGill-Queen's University Press. 1753-1835. http://www.jstor.org/stable/j.ctt130hgg4

Bibliography

Marsh, J. Sex & sexuality in the 19th Century. Victoria and Albert Museum, London. http://www.vam.ac.uk/content/articles/s/sex-and-sexuality-19th-century/

Blakemore, E. (October, 2017). The scandalous sex parties that made Americans hate flappers. https://www.history.com/news/the-scandalous-sex-parties-that-made-americans-hate-flappers

The Kinsey Institute. Learn our history. https://kinseyinstitute.org/about/history/alfred-kinsey.php

Flexner, E. (1996). Century of struggle: The woman's rights movement in the United States. Paperback Edition, Belknap Press.

Sanger, M. (1938). Margaret Sanger: An autobiography. W. W. Norton. 361, 366–7.

History.com Editors. (February, 2019). Women's history milestones: A timeline. https://www.history.com/topics/womens-history/womens-history-us-timeline

Nikolchev, A. (May, 2010). A brief history of the birth control pill. PBS. https://www.pbs.org/wnet/need-to-know/health/a-brief-history-of-the-birth-control-pill/480/

OBOS Birth Control Contributors. (2013, 2020). A brief history of birth control in the U.S. https://www.

ourbodiesourselves.org/book-excerpts/health-article/a-brief-history-of-birth-control/

Schneir, M. (1994). Feminism: The essential historical writings. Vintage. ISBN 0-679-75381-8

CHAPTER 2

Intelligence. In Merriam-Webster Dictionary. https://www.merriam-webster.com/dictionary/intelligence

Davitz, J. R. (1976). The communication of emotional meaning. Greenwood Pub Group.

Fancher, R. E. (1983). Biographical origins of Francis Galton's psychology. Isis, 74(2), 227–233. doi:10.1086/353245.

Schmidt, F. L., & Hunter, J. E. (1998). The validity and utility of selection methods in personnel psychology: Practical and theoretical implications of 85 years of research findings. Psychological Bulletin. 124(2), 262–74.

Goleman, D., & Boyatzis, R. E. (February, 2017). Emotional Intelligence has 12 elements.:Which do you need to work on? https://hbr.org/2017/02/emotional-intelligence-has-12-elements-which-do-you-need-to-work-on

Goleman, D. (1995). Emotional Intelligence: Why It Can Matter More Than IQ. Bantam.

Bibliography

Klein, M. (2012). Sexual Intelligence: What we really want from sex--and how to get it. Harper Collins.

Perel, E. (2006). Dating in captivity: Unlocking erotic intelligence. Harper Collins.

CHAPTER 3

Dickler, J. (March, 2018). #TimesUp changes workplace relationships well beyond Hollywood. CNBC. https://www.cnbc.com/2018/03/05/times-up-changes-workplace-relationships-well-beyond-hollywood.html

Kohll, A. (August, 2018). How to build a positive company culture. Forbes. https://www.forbes.com/sites/alankohll/2018/08/14/how-to-build-a-positive-company-culture/?sh=664848a549b5

Romance in the workplace: It's happening, but is it allowed? Romance in the workplace. (June, 2019). CNW Group/ADP Canada. https://www.newswire.ca/news-releases/romance-in-the-workplace-it-s-happening-but-is-it-allowed--894172931.html

Flanagan, K. (July, 2019). The problem with HR. The Atlantic. https://www.theatlantic.com/magazine/archive/2019/07/hr-workplace-harrassment-me-too/590644/

Feldblulm, C. R., & Lipnic, V. A. (June, 2016). Report: US Equal Employment Opportunity Commission.

Select Task Force on the Study of Harassment in the Workplace. https://www.eeoc.gov/select-task-force-study-harassment-workplace

Chinery, A. (November, 2020). Love from 9 to 5: Office romance statistics. Reboot Online. https://www.rebootonline.com/blog/office-relations-study/

16 percent of people met their spouse at work. (February, 2016). Business Insider. https://www.businessinsider.com/surprising-office-romance-statistics-2016-2

Elsesser, K. (February, 2019). These 6 surprising office romance stats should be a wake-up call for organizations. Forbes. https://www.forbes.com/sites/kimelsesser/2019/02/14/these-6-surprising-office-romance-stats-should-be-a-wake-up-call-to-organizations/?sh=4314c1a623a2

CHAPTER 4

Carlsen, A., Salam, M., Cain MIller, C., Lu, D., Ngu, A., Patel, J. K., & Wichter, Z. (2018). #MeToo brought down 201 powerful men. Nearly half of their replacements are women., updated October 29, 2018, New York Times. https://www.nytimes.com/interactive/2018/10/23/us/metoo-replacements.html

Sexual Harassment, Employment and Social Development Canada. https://www.canada.ca/en/

employment-social-development/services/labour-standards/reports/sexual-harassment.html

Collins, E. G. C. & Blodgett, T. B. (March, 1981). Sexual harassment...Some see it...wome won't. Harvard Business Review. https://hbr.org/1981/03/sexual-harassmentsome-see-itsome-wont

Ventura, S. J., & Bachrach, C. A. (2000). Nonmarital childbearing in the United States, 1940-99. National Vital Statistics Reports. Centers for Disease Control and Prevention, 48(16), 1-40. https://www.cdc.gov/Nchs/data/nvsr/nvsr48/nvs48_16.pdf

Tenenbaum, L. (January, 2018). Celebrated author Margaret Atwood challenges #MeToo's lynch mob justice. WSWS. https://www.wsws.org/en/articles/2018/01/23/meto-j23.html

Atwater, L. E., Tringale, A. M., Sturm, R. E., Taylor, S. N., & Braddy, P. W. (2019). Looking ahead: How what we know about sexual harassment now informs us of the future. Organizational Dynamics, 48(4). https://doi.org/10.1016/j.orgdyn.2018.08.008.

Deschamps, T. (2018). #MeToo backlash in corporate Canada sees women locked out. Huffington Post. https://www.huffingtonpost.ca/2018/08/02/metoo-backlash-corporate-canada_a_23494668/

Bower, T. (September-October, 2019). The #MeToo Backlash. Harvard Business Review. https://hbr.org/2019/09/the-metoo-backlash

DailyMail.com Reporter. (August, 2019). Men now AVOID women at work and are much more reluctant to shake a female colleague's hand or hire an attractive woman because of #MeToo, study finds. Daily Mail UK. https://www.dailymail.co.uk/news/article-7408599/Men-avoid-women-work-sign-punished-MeToo.html

Tan, G., & Porzecanski, K. (December, 2018). Wall Street rule for the #MeToo Era: Avoid women at all cost. Bloomberg. https://www.bloomberg.com/news/articles/2018-12-03/a-wall-street-rule-for-the-metoo-era-avoid-women-at-all-cost

Deschamps, T. (August, 2018). Women locked out of old boys' club in misguided #MeToo backlash. The Canadian Press. https://www.thestar.com/business/2018/08/02/women-locked-out-of-old-boys-club-in-misguided-metoo-backlash.html

Kenny, M. (November, 2017) I used to hear men say that "only tarts kiss and tell"', Am I a Feminist'? Are you'? TheJournal.ie. https://www.thejournal.ie/readme/mary-kenny-i-used-to-hear-men-say-that-only-tarts-kiss-and-tell-3678510-Nov2017/

Xenakis, C. (March, 2019). Avoiding women at all cost: The #MeToo backlash and boundary awareness chauvinism in the Church. https://carducc.wordpress.com/2019/03/04/avoiding-women-at-all-cost-the-metoo-backlash/

Paglia, C. (2017). Free women, free men: Sex, gender, feminism. Pantheon.

CHAPTER 5

Galinsky, A. (March, 2018). Are gender differences just power differences in disguise? Columbia Business School. https://www8.gsb.columbia.edu/articles/ideas-work/are-gender-differences-just-power-differences-disguise

Patriarchy. In Lexico. https://www.lexico.com/en/definition/patriarchy

Foucault, M. (1976). The history of sexuality. Editions Gallimard.

Zheng, W., Kark, R., & Meister, A. (November, 2018). How women manage the gendered norms of leadership. Harvard Business Review. https://hbr.org/2018/11/how-women-manage-the-gendered-norms-of-leadership

Wilson Schaef, A. (1992). Women's reality: An emerging female system in a white male society. Harper San Francisco.

Paglia, C. (2017). Free women, free men: Sex, gender, feminism. Pantheon.

Patriarchy. In Merriam-Webster Dictionary. https://www.merriam-webster.com/dictionary/patriarchy

Gilligan, C., & Snider, N. (October, 2018). Why does patriarchy persist? Athena Reads. https://athenareads.home.blog/2018/07/31/why-does-patriarchy-persist/ de Beauvoir, S. (1949). Le deuxième sexe [The Second Sex]. Gallimard.

Beau, E. (November, 2018). The history of patriarchy: It's not about men; it's a social system that is only 10K years old. Medium. https://medium.com/inside-of-elle-beau/the-history-of-patriarchy-5ed57240a2bb

Hooks, B. (2004). The will to change: Men, masculinity, and love. Atria.

Ananthaswamy, A., & Douglas, K. (April, 2018). The origins of sexism: How men came to rule 12,000 years ago. New Scientist. https://www.newscientist.com/article/mg23831740-400-the-origins-of-sexism-how-men-came-to-rule-12000-years-ago/

Kilianski, S. E., & Rudman, L. (1998). Wanting it both ways: Do women approve of benevolent sexism? Sex Roles, 39(5), 333-352. doi: 10.1023/A:1018814924402 https://www.researchgate.net/publication/251261112

Bibliography

_Wanting_It_Both_Ways_Do_Women_Approve_of_Benevolent_Sexism

Glick, P., & Fiske, S. T. (2001). An ambivalent alliance, hostile and benevolent sexism as complementary justifications for gender inequality. American Psychologist, 56(2), 109-118. https://www.researchgate.net/profile/Peter_Glick/publication/12053318_An_Ambivalent_Alliance_Hostile_and_Benevolent_Sexism_as_Complementary_Justifications_for_Gender_Inequality/links/00b4952e699935d24e000000.pdf

CHAPTER 6

Kray L. J., Locke C. C., & Van Zant A.B. (2012) Feminine charm: An experimental analysis of its costs and benefits in negotiations. Personality and Social Psychology Bulletin, 38(10), 1343-1357. doi: 10.1177/0146167212453074

Study finds flirting can pay off for women. (October, 2012). Berkeley Haas News. https://newsroom.haas.berkeley.edu/study-finds-flirting-can-pay-women-negotiations/

Gutlove, P. (2012). Flirting with negotiation — Redefining 'feminine charm'. Huffington Post. https://www.huffpost.com/entry/flirting-with-negotiation_b_2094668

O'Connell, B. (October, 2012). Flirting pays off In the workplace, study says (but women only). The Street.

https://www.thestreet.com/investing/stocks/flirting-pays-off-in-the-workplace-study-says-but-women-only-11740091

Locke, C. (March, 2016). Is flirtation an effective negotiation tactic? London School of Economics and Political Science. https://blogs.lse.ac.uk/management/2016/03/28/is-flirtation-an-effective-negotiation-tactic/

Artz, B., Goodall, A., & Oswald, A. J. (2018). Research: Women ask for raises as often as men, but are less likely to get them. Harvard Business Review. https://hbr.org/2018/06/research-women-ask-for-raises-as-often-as-men-but-are-less-likely-to-get-them

Williams, J. C. (August, 2019). How women can escape the likability trap. The New York Times. https://www.nytimes.com/2019/08/16/opinion/sunday/gender-bias-work.html

Matar, J. (April, 1014). Here's the secret to negotiating with the opposite sex. Brazen. https://www.brazen.com/blog/archive/career-growth/heres-secret-negotiating-opposite-sex

Mazei, J., Hüffmeier, J., Freund, P. A., Stuhlmacher, A. F., Bilke, L., & Hertel, G. (2015). A meta-analysis on gender differences in negotiation outcomes and their moderators. Psychological Bulletin, 141(1), 85-104. doi:10.1037/a0038184.

Bibliography

Kray, L.J., & Kennedy, J. A. (2017). Changing the narrative: Women as negotiators—and leaders. California Management Review, 60(1), 70-87. doi:10.1177/0008125617727744

Hunter Murray, S. (June, 2017). How masculinity is stifling men's sexual desire. https://www.sarahhuntermurray.com/myths-of-desire/2017/6/21/how-masculinity-is-stifling-mens-sexual-desire

Mirvis, P. (2012). Employee engagement and CSR: Transactional, relational, and developmental approaches. California Management Review, 54, 93-117. 10.1525/cmr.2012.54.4.93.

Dunning, D. (June, 2017). We Are All Confident Idiots, The trouble with ignorance is that it feels so much like expertise. A leading researcher on the psychology of human wrongness sets us straight. Pacific Standard Magazine. https://psmag.com/social-justice/confident-idiots-92793

De Janasz, S. & Cabrera, B. (August, 2018). How women can get what they want in a negotiation. Harvard Business Review. https://hbr.org/2018/08/how-women-can-get-what-they-want-in-a-negotiation

CHAPTER 7

Lederach, J. (1996). Preparing for peace: Conflict transformation across cultures. Syracuse University Press.

Maslow, A. H. (1943). A theory of human motivation. Psychological Review, 50(4), 370-96.

Weir, K. (February, 2017). The men America left behind. Monitor on Psychology, 48(2). http://www.apa.org/monitor/2017/02/men-left-behind

K for Kira. (August, 2019). Men matter too. Medium. https://medium.com/@kiramamula/men-matter-too-dont-they-b47cb9c15970

Iwamoto, D. K., Brady, J., Kaya, A., & Park, A. (2018). Masculinity and depression: A longitudinal investigation of multidimensional masculine norms among college men. American Journal of Men's Health, 12(6), 1873–1881. https://doi.org/10.1177/1557988318785549

Wong, Y. J., Ho, M.-H. R., Wang, S.-Y., & Miller, I. S. K. (2017). Meta-analyses of the relationship between conformity to masculine norms and mental health-related outcomes. Journal of Counseling Psychology, 64(1), 80–93. https://doi.org/10.1037/cou0000176 https://www.apa.org/news/press/releases/2016/11/sexism-harmful

Mozes, A. (November, 2016). Being sexist could harm men's health, study suggests. CBS News. https://www.cbsnews.com/news/being-sexist-could-harm-mens-health-study/

Paella, G. (November, 2016). Sexism can be harmful for Men Too, but not in the ways you might think. The Cut. https://www.thecut.com/2016/11/study-links-sexism-to-poor-mental-health-for-men.html

O'Neill, J. M. (November, 2014). Men's gender role conflict: Psychological costs, consequences, and an agenda for change. American Psychological Association.

Cassino, D. (April, 2017). Earning less than their wives makes U.S. men more partisan. Harvard Business Review. https://hbr.org/2017/04/earning-less-than-their-wives-makes-u-s-men-more-partisan

Samuels, T. (2017). Who stole my spear? Century.

Vanvuren, C. (April, 2018). Illuminating the double standards of parenthood. Blood and Milk. https://www.bloodandmilk.com/illuminating-the-double-standards-of-parenthood/

Raising kids and running a household: How working parents share the load. (November, 2015). Pew Research Center. https://www.pewsocialtrends.org/2015/11/04/raising-kids-and-running-a-household-how-working-parents-share-the-load/

Telegraph Men. (November, 2014). 'A crisis of masculinity': Men are struggling to cope with life. Telegraph.

https://www.telegraph.co.uk/men/thinking-man/11238596/A-crisis-of-masculinity-men-are-struggling-to-cope-with-life.html

Powell, J. (November, 2014). A crisis in modern masculinity: Understanding the causes of male suicide. The Calm Zone. https://www.thecalmzone.net/wp-content/uploads/2014/11/CALM-State-of-the-Nation-Audit-Summary.pdf

This survey was designed by Public Knowledge in collaboration with CALM and representatives from their Year of the Male Steering Group; Damien Ridge (University of Westminster), Steve Robertson (Leeds Metropolitan Uni), Martin Todd (Men's Health Forum), Martin Seager (Consultant Clinical Psychologist), John Barry (Chartered Psychologist), activist Glen Poole (Editor at insideMAN magazine) and advice from the Young Foundation.

Daye Scott, S. (August, 2017). Girl power has lifted up women but failed men. Washington Post. https://www.chicagotribune.com/lifestyles/ct-girl-power-failing-men-20170829-story.html

"All conflicts are identity conflicts..." -- John Paul Lederach.

"As we uncover our true nature, we realize all those things we have attached to our identity are merely labels to realize that a sense of place in the world.

Moreover, I create a false sense of self to form an image of who they think I am. Discarding the false self is a call to abandon the beliefs and thoughts of who you think you are in discovering a stronger sense of self". - Tony Fahrky, Mission.org

"True self is non-self, the awareness that the self is made only of non-self elements. There's no separation between self and other, and everything is interconnected. Once you are aware of that, you are no longer caught in the idea that you are a separate entity." — Thich Nhat Hanh.

"You wouldn't worry so much about what others think of you if you realized how seldom they do," said Eleanor Roosevelt, American politician and activist.

CHAPTER 8

Fisher, T. D., Moore, Z. T., & Pittenger, M. (2012). Sex on the brain? An examination of frequency of sexual cognitions as a function of gender, erotophilia, and social desirability. Journal of Sex Research, 29, 69-77. doi: 10.1080/00224499.2011.565429

Hobbs D. R., & Gallup, G. G. (2011). Songs as a medium for embedded reproductive messages. Evolutionary Psychology. doi:10.1177/147470491100900309

Grandoni, D. (September, 2011). 92% of Top Ten Billboard Songs are about sex, "Sex appeal," "arousal," and "other body parts" are popular themes in American music. The Atlantic. https://www.theatlantic.com/culture/archive/2011/09/92-top-ten-billboard-songs-are-about-sex/337242/

Urbani, D. (1999). Can regular sex ward off colds and flu? Results from study conducted by Charnetski and Brennon, presented at a meeting of the Eastern Psychological Association in Providence, Rhode Island. https://www.newscientist.com/article/mg16221820-800-can-regular-sex-ward-off-colds-and-flu/

Urbani, D. (1999). Sex can boost the immune system (1999). New Scientist. newscientist.com/article/mg16221820-800-can-regular-sex-ward-off-colds-and-flu/ Reported at: https://www.eurekalert.org/pub_releases/1999-04/NS-SCBT-140499.php

Barman, L., & Barman, J. (2001). For women only: A revolutionary guide to reclaiming your sex life. Henry Holt and Co.

7 surprising joys of sex: Health benefits. (April 2013). My Take On Today. https://mytakeontoday.wordpress.com/tag/sandor-gardos/

Healthy pelvic health leads to better sexual life. Vibrance. https://vibrance.com.my/healthy-pelvic-health-leads-to-better-sexual-life

Morales, C. (February, 2018). Why sex is important in a relationship support your marriage—have sex.

Bibliography

Fine Homes and Living. https://www.finehomesandliving.com/featured/why-sex-is-important-in-a-relationship/article_a9bf2312-c9c5-5422-8910-7fe2e6bd2484.html

Jovanovic, J. (2019). 21 reasons why sex is important. ALLWOMENSTALK. https://allwomenstalk.com/7-reasons-why-sex-is-important/

Bachai, S. (2013). The top 10 reasons why sex is good for you. Medical Daily. https://www.medicaldaily.com/top-10-reasons-why-sex-good-you-246020

Wright, H., Jenks, R. A., & Demeyere, N. (2019). Frequent sexual activity predicts specific cognitive abilities in older adults. The Journals of Gerontology. Series B, Psychological Sciences and Social Sciences, 74(1), 47-51. doi:10.1093/geronb/gbx065 https://www.ncbi.nlm.nih.gov/pmc/articles/PMC6294227/

Wu, K (2017). Love, actually: The science behind lust, attraction, and companionship. Harvard University School of Arts and Sciences. http://sitn.hms.harvard.edu/flash/2017/love-actually-science-behind-lust-attraction-companionship/

Fisher, H. (2005). Why we love: The nature and chemistry of romantic love. Holt Paperbacks.

Your Brain on Love. BrainHQ. https://www.brainhq.com/brain-resources/cool-brain-facts-myths/brain-in-love/

Watson, R. (2013). Oxytocin: The love and trust hormone can be deceptive. Psychology Today. https://www.psychologytoday.com/ca/blog/love-and-gratitude/201310/oxytocin-the-love-and-trust-hormone-can-be-deceptive

Estima, S. (April, 2018). Why women need twice as much sex as men. https://thriveglobal.com/stories/why-women-need-twice-as-much-sex-as-men/

Breaux, J. (November, 2009). What is the flow state. San Diego Entertainer Magazine. https://www.sdentertainer.com/lifestyle/what-is-the-flow-state/

Kennedy, A. (2016). Flow state: What it is and how to achieve it. Huffington Post. https://www.huffpost.com/entry/flow-state-what-it-is-and_b_9607084

Csikszentmihalyi, M. (1998). Finding flow: The psychology of engagement with everyday life. Basic Books.

Csikszentmihalyi, M. (1990). Flow: The psychology of optimal experience. Harper & Row.

Chamberlin, K. (2016). This Scientific Study Could Rock Your Sexual World in the Best Possible Way. https://www.thehealthy.com/sex/sex-trace-like-state/

Bibliography

Safron, A. (2016). What is orgasm? A model of sexual trance and climax via rhythmic entrainment. Socioaffective Neuroscience & Psychology, 6, 31763. doi:10.3402/snp.v6.31763

CHAPTER 9

Femme Fatale. In Merriam-Webster Dictionary. https://www.merriam-webster.com/dictionary/femme%20fatale

James, L. (February, 2020). The femme fatale: A brief history of beauty as a surprisingly effective legal defense. Crime Reads. https://crimereads.com/the-femme-fatale-a-brief-history-of-beauty-as-a-surprisingly-effective-legal-defense/

Barber, N. (2014). Sin City's Eva Green and femme fatales' sexy history. BBC. https://www.bbc.com/culture/article/20140821-femme-fatale-a-sexy-history

Hanson, H., & O'Rawe, C. (2010). The femme fatale: Images, histories, contexts. Palgrave Macmillan UK. https://doi.org/10.1057/9780230282018 https://link.springer.com/book/10.1057%2F9780230282018#about

Pettit, C. (November, 2012). 10 real life femme fatales through the ages. GuySpeed. https://guyspeed.com/10-real-life-femme-fatales-through-the-ages/

Andrews, S. (April, 2017). Femme Fatales: Scandalous women of history who changed society around them. The Vintage News. https://www.thevintagenews.com/2017/04/14/femme-fatales-scandalous-women-of-history-who-changed-society-around-them/

CHAPTER 10

Campos, P. F. (January, 2013). Our absurd fear of fat. The New York Times. https://www.nytimes.com/2013/01/03/opinion/our-imaginary-weight-problem.html

Flegal, K. M., Kit, B. K., Orpana, H., & Graubard, B. I. (2013). Association of all-cause mortality with overweight and obesity using Standard Body Mass Index categories: A systematic review and meta-analysis. JAMA, 309(1), 71–82. doi:10.1001/jama.2012.113905

Talley, H. L. (2017). The ugly side of lookism and what we can do about it. Huffington Post. https://www.huffpost.com/entry/the-ugly-side-of-lookism_b_9042114

Griffin, A. M., & Langlois, J. H. (2006). Stereotype Directionality and Attractiveness Stereotyping: Is Beauty Good or is Ugly Bad?. Social Cognition, 24(2), 187-206. doi:10.1521/soco.2006.24.2.187

Cherry, K. (2020). What is the Halo Effect? Very Well Mind. https://www.verywellmind.com/what-is-the-halo-effect-2795906

Bibliography

Thorndike, E.L. (1920). A constant error in psychological ratings. Journal of Applied Psychology, 4(1), 25–29. https://doi.org/10.1037/h0071663

White, A. E., & Kenrick, D. T. (2013) Why attractive candidates win. The New York Times. https://www.nytimes.com/2013/11/03/opinion/sunday/health-beauty-and-the-ballot.html

White, A. E., Kenrick, D. T., & Neuberg, S. L. (2013). Beauty at the ballot box: Disease threats predict Preferences for physically attractive leaders. Psychological Science, 24(12), 2429-2436. doi:10.1177/0956797613493642

Maner, J. K., & Kenrick, D. T. (2010). When adaptations go awry: Functional and dysfunctional aspects of social anxiety. Social Issues and Policy Review, 4(1), 111–142. https://doi.org/10.1111/j.1751-2409.2010.01019.x

Mobius, M. M., & Rosenblat, T. S. (2006). Why beauty matters. American Economic Review, 96(1), 222-235. https://dash.harvard.edu/handle/1/3043406

Slater, A., Quinn, P. C., Kelly, D. J., Lee, K., Longmore, C. A., McDonald, P. R., & Pascalis, O. (2010). The shaping of the face space in early infancy: Becoming a native face processor. Child Development Perspectives, 4(3), 205–211. https://doi.org/10.1111/j.1750-8606.2010.00147.x

Barber, N. (July, 2018). Why looks still matter as women gain power. https://www.psychologytoday.com/ca/blog/the-human-beast/201807/why-looks-still-matter-women-gain-power

Jackson, L. (1992). Physical appearance and gender: Sociobiological and sociocultural perspectives. State University of New York Press.

Gosline, A. (2004). Babies prefer to gaze upon beautiful faces. New Scientist. https://www.newscientist.com/article/dn6355-babies-prefer-to-gaze-upon-beautiful-faces

Lister, K. (September, 2018). The male beauty pageant where female judges sleep with the winners. VICE. https://www.vice.com/en_uk/article/a383vk/the-male-beauty-pageant-where-female-judges-sleep-with-the-winners

Hilder, L. (October, 2003). Abs make the heart grow fonder. The Guardian. https://www.theguardian.com/world/2003/oct/26/gender

Hilton, L. S. (March, 2016). Time to be grown up about female desire. The Guardian. https://www.theguardian.com/commentisfree/2016/mar/06/lisa-hilton-maestra-book-sex-women

Parrett, M. (2015). Beauty and the feast: Examining the effect of beauty on earnings using restaurant tipping data. Journal of Economic Psychology, 49, 34-46. doi:10.1016/j.joep.2015.04.002

Craig, L., & Gray, P. (2020). Women's use of intimate apparel as subtle sexual signals in committed, heterosexual relationships. PLoS One, 15(3), e0230112.

Etcoff, N. (2000). Survival of the prettiest: The science of beauty. Anchor.

Popova, M. (July, 2013). Survival of the prettiest: Harvard cognitive scientist Nancy Etcoff on the science of beauty. Brain Pickings https://www.brainpickings.org/2013/07/01/survival-of-the-prettiest-nancy-ectoff/

Etcoff, N. L., Stock, S., Haley, L. E., Vickery, S. A., & House, D. M. (2011). Cosmetics as a feature of the extended human phenotype: modulation of the perception of biologically important facial signals. PLoS One, 6(10), e25656. doi: 10.1371/journal.pone.0025656.

Hamermesh, D. (2011). Beauty pays: Why attractive people are more successful. Princeton University Press.

Judge, T. A., Hurst, C., & Simon, L. S. (2009). Does it pay to be smart, attractive, or confident (or all three)? Relationships among general mental ability, physical attractiveness, core self-evaluations and income. Journal of Applied Psychology, 94(3), 742-755. doi:10.1037/a0015497

MacDonald, F. (May, 2015). Wearing a suit changes the way your brain works. Science Alert. https://www.sciencealert.com/research-shows-wearing-a-suit-changes-the-way-you-think

Slepian, M. L., Ferber, S. N., Gold, J. M., & Rutchick, A. M. (2015). The cognitive consequences of formal clothing. Social Psychological and Personality Science. 6. doi:10.1111/j.1559-1816.2004.tb01987.xCorpus ID: 39081993

Etcoff, N. L., Stock, S., Haley, L. E., Vickery, S. A., & House, D. M. (2011). Cosmetics as a feature of the extended human phenotype: modulation of the perception of biologically important facial signals. PLoS One, 6(10), e25656. doi: 10.1371/journal.pone.0025656.

Slepian, M. L., Ferber, S. N., Gold, J. M., & Rutchick, A. M. (2015). The cognitive consequences of formal clothing. Social and Personality Psychology Science, 6, 661-668. doi:10.1111/j.1559-1816.2004.tb01987.xCorpus ID: 39081993

Brase, G. L., & Richmond, J. M. (2004). The white-coat effect: Physician attire and perceived authority, friendliness, and attractiveness. Journal of Applied Social Psychology, 34(12), 2469-2481.

Sorvino, C. (May, 2017). Why the $445 billion beauty industry is a gold mine for self-made women. Forbes. https://www.forbes.com/sites/chloesorvino/2017/05/18/self-made-women-wealth-beauty-gold-mine/

Global cosmetic surgery and service market report 2015-2019 - Analysis of the $27 billion industry. PR Newswire https://www.prnewswire.com/news-releases/global-cosmetic-surgery-and-service-market-report-2015-2019---analysis-of-the-27-billion-industry-300053760.html

The state of fashion 2021. McKinsey. https://www.mckinsey.com/industries/retail/our-insights/state-of-fashion

CHAPTER 11

Castillo, M. (August, 2013). Study: People who have sex four or more times a week make more money. CBS News. https://www.cbsnews.com/news/study-people-who-have-sex-four-or-more-times-a-week-make-more-money/

Drydakis, N. (July, 2013). The Effect of Sexual Activity on Wages. IZA Discussion Paper No. 7529. Institute for the Study of Labor. Bonn, Germany. http://ftp.iza.org/dp7529.pdf

Hill, N. (1937). Think and grow rich. Chump Change.

Garnett, L. (February, 2016). 3 reasons more sex will bring you more success. Inc. https://www.inc.com/laura-garnett/3-reasons-more-sex-will-bring-you-more-success.html

Meepagala, R. Sex transmutation: How to channel sex energy to fascinate, attract abundance, and create your reality. Fearless. https://www.thefearlessman.com/sex-transmutation-how-to-channel-sex-energy-to-fascinate-attract-abundance-and-create-your-reality/

Lehmiller, J. (June, 2018). We looked into whether having sex affects your athletic performance. https://www.vice.com/en/article/d3keaq/we-looked-into-whether-having-sex-affects-your-athletic-performance

Reiners, B. (October, 2019). What is gender bias in the workplace? Built In. https://builtin.com/diversity-inclusion/gender-bias-in-the-workplace

Lockhard, B. (May, 2016). I use my sexuality to get ahead at work, and I don't feel bad about it. https://thefinancialdiet.com/use-sexuality-get-ahead-work-dont-feel-bad/

Hakim, C. (2011). Honey money: The power Of erotic capital. Allen Lane.

Bibliography

Brick, S. (August, 2011). I use my sex appeal to get ahead at work… and so does ANY woman with any sense. Daily Mail UK. https://www.dailymail.co.uk/femail/article-2029781/I-use-sex-appeal-ahead-work--does-ANY-woman-sense.html

Dugan, C. (February, 2017). Why Shark Tank's Barbara Corcoran 'chose to ignore the female card totally' in the workplace. https://people.com/tv/shark-tank-barbara-corcoran-ignore-female-card-workplace-advice/

Paglia, C. (2017). Free women, free men: Sex, gender, feminism. Pantheon.

Printed in Great Britain
by Amazon